What People Are Saying About

The Art of Sensing

The Art of Sensing is a clearly written guide that illuminates the process of spiritual transformation that frequently arises through experiencing life difficulties. Carole Obley uses examples from her numerous case files of mediumship readings to illustrate how tough times help us to grow beyond who we *think* we are to who we truly are.

George Noory, host of *Coast to Coast* radio

This book offers both a banquet and a roadmap complete with pathways and bridges to take you on a journey toward the proverbial pot of gold — your timeless, eternal, immutable, ineffable, omniscient Self — the fundamental truth of who you are. The pathways are clearly marked. Only one thing stands in the way, your own fear. *The Art of Sensing* guides you through that too. Ms. Obley is clear: This journey is your reason for being here.

Susan Plunket, author of *A Jungian Understanding of Transcendent Experiences*

I've seen Carole Obley in action and have been amazed by her psychic gifts! She brings her spiritual insight back to the written page in this new book which takes the mystery out of soul work and teaches us how to persevere in the face of personal challenges. Knowledge is power. Discover how to seize it by reading *The Art of Sensing* today!

Jim Harold, host of *The Paranormal Podcast* and *Jim Harold's Campfire*

T0343667

Carole Obley delivers the urgent and profound message for humanity to journey within and connect with the Higher Self. This book serves as a guide, offering a rich array of tools to access the dormant aspects within each of us that are begging to awaken. This book will encourage you to embark on the inner journey, exploring the depths of your consciousness. Carole draws from her years of experience, providing an abundance of wisdom and guidance. Her exploration spans across time and space, revealing the keys to unlocking your true sense of soul.
Shanna Vavra, host of *Sense of Soul Podcast*

Obley offers real-life stories from her numerous case files that will inspire people to transcend difficulties. *The Art of Sensing* is a book we all need to read, more now than ever. A triumph!
G.L. Davies, author of *Haunted: Horror of Haverfordwest*

The Art of Sensing

A Guide for Staying True to Your Soul's
Journey through Challenging Times

The Art of Sensing

A Guide for Staying True to Your Soul's
Journey through Challenging Times

carole j. obley

**6TH
BOOKS**

London, UK
Washington, DC, USA

CollectiveInk

First published by Sixth Books, 2025
Sixth Books is an imprint of Collective Ink Ltd.,
Unit 11, Shepperton House, 89 Shepperton Road, London, N1 3DF
office@collectiveinkbooks.com
www.collectiveinkbooks.com
www.6th-books.com

For distributor details and how to order please visit the 'Ordering' section on our website.

Design: Lapiz Digital Services

UK: Printed and bound by CPI Group (UK) Ltd, Croydon, CR0 4YY
Printed in North America by CPI GPS partners

This book is not intended as a substitute for professional medical advice. The reader should
consult the appropriate healthcare professional regarding specific needs. All client names used
herein are pseudonyms to protect privacy.

We operate a distinctive and ethical publishing philosophy in
all areas of our business, from our global network of authors to
production and worldwide distribution.

Contents

To all those who seek the Light within;
and to Embers,
who taught me to love without expectation of return.

Introduction

There is no time, no place, no state where God is
absent. There is nothing to be feared.
~*A Course in Miracles*

It's a balmy Saturday evening in mid-September 1968. I'm 10 years old and carefully rolling my hair in curlers for church the following morning as Mom and I watch the annual Miss America Pageant on our new color TV. We're captivated by the talent competition for the 12 finalists and Miss Alabama is on stage.

I listen intently as the emcee explains that the contestant is studying to be an interpreter for the deaf. Flashing a bright smile, Miss Alabama proceeds to demonstrate her sign language abilities, deftly moving her hands and fingers in synch with the emcee's narration. I'm mesmerized by the fluid expressiveness of this silent language. Something (I have no idea what) suddenly clicks in my head. I have chills, tingles, goosebumps and a feeling of "knowing."

"That's what I want to do when I grow up, Mom!" I squeal, pointing excitedly at the screen. "Yes! That is something I would *really* like to do! She's helping people who can't hear to understand what the man is saying!"

I have no conscious idea why I feel this way but what I sense is real, compelling, striking, and startling.

Mom, seemingly unimpressed, remains fixated on the TV and says nothing. She gives me a sidelong glance, similar to when I'd asked for a new doll. But her lack of acknowledging my announcement doesn't matter; I *feel* it in my heart. Actually, it goes deeper than my heart. It permeates to my bones, to the very fabric of my being. What I do not realize in these moments is that this incident represents my first conscious awareness of my soul speaking directly to me.

Decades later, it occurred to me that the resonance I felt with the deaf interpreter was an early intuitive recognition of my soul's journey into mediumship. I made the connection between the two: the interpreter (who hears spoken words) using her skills to help those who cannot hear those words.

Likewise, as a medium, I use my skills to relay communication that I hear from souls in spirit to those in the physical world who cannot "hear." Once I understood this, it was as if a bright light came on: At age 10, my soul was setting the stage for my life's work by giving me promptings and reminders of what I had planned to do before birth. Although not consciously recalled in most instances, these blueprints for life are part of the *akashic files*, and are made by our soul before coming into the physical world. The files consist of the past, present, and possible future consciousness of souls. I address more about this in Chapter One.

During childhood, I'd had no exposure to the phenomenon of mediumship. Ours was a church-centered household and the paranormal was not a topic of conversation. I'm convinced that my visceral response to the beauty pageant performance on TV that night was foreshadowing what was to eventually unfold in my adult life. It was a soul wakeup call that reverberated within the deepest part of my being, triggered by a mundane external event.

Although it took many years to embrace my calling — after struggles with addiction, recovery and a catastrophic fire — I ultimately stepped onto the path of mediumship during my late 30s. Yet the soul knows nothing of time; it simply expresses itself. Its eternal light and wisdom are never extinguished but securely anchored within the body, the vehicle that houses it.

Expanding Your Senses to Include Your Sixth Sense

Perhaps you, too, have received clues about the direction of your life. Maybe it was an experience similar to mine where something you encountered inexplicably resonated with you through your senses. Or perhaps you've had to confront a challenging illness, cope with childhood trauma, grieve a close loved one's passing, end an unhealthy relationship, or leave an unfulfilling career. Perhaps you didn't know which way to turn — until you surrendered to the guidance of your soul.

On the flip side, perhaps you found the perfect mate, the dream career that meets your heart's desires, endearing friends, or personal fulfillment in service to others. Whatever your case, there is one common denominator among all of these experiences: By following your "gut feeling" and despite the uncertainty of the outcome, you took the initial step to realize your soul's need to move, change and grow. When you recall how you've navigated these circumstances, you may now recognize that your soul was leading you to experience wholeness, fulfillment, and peace from the start. You moved through doubt and fear to trust the process by taking the first step on the journey. This is a direct demonstration of how courageous you are. This is proof of your determination to move forward and follow the wisdom of your inner being. Significantly, this is how you will *continue* your journey when times are tough, challenging, and seemingly hopeless.

This is a book about courageously following the pathway of your soul during difficult, uncertain times by trusting its guidance as it manifests through your sixth sense — namely, your intuition. Throughout the chapters, you will find clear instructions on how to distinguish your soul's intuitive calling from your rational mind, societal expectations, and ingrained thought patterns. In doing so, you will gain clarity of purpose by successfully rising above fear. You'll recognize difficulties and challenges for what they are: windows of opportunity to evolve spiritually. You'll discover useful practices to open, develop and, importantly, *trust* that inner voice. I recommend doing these exercises often and in order because they build upon one another. Additionally, you'll read stories of others who have endured difficult passages in their lives and how these led them to spiritual transformation.

As in my earlier books, the inspiration for this one was gleaned from thousands of sessions with clients in my practice of professional mediumship, workshop presentations, in-depth studies of astrology, and my own personal journey through decades of working with higher consciousness. This work has provided me with myriad insights about the nature of the soul and its journey in both the physical and spirit worlds, as well as its elevated consciousness, apart from the rational mind.

Each chapter features anecdotes from multiple client sessions that illustrate key concepts about the soul, intuition, and spiritual consciousness. I have done numerous sittings with individuals who've suffered immeasurable grief from losing a child, those who've faced serious illnesses, and others who've carried the profound wounds of childhood abuse. In these sessions and many others, people were able to connect with the higher wisdom of Spirit from their own soul. My role as a medium is to impart that wisdom as clearly and accurately as possible, knowing that I am not the source of it, merely the conduit.

In previous writings and in various media interviews, I've mentioned that the number one question people ask during readings is *What is my purpose?* Embedded within that question are others: *What is the meaning (in a spiritual sense) of my life? Why did a particular painful event happen to me? How can I successfully take charge of my life? How do I get "there" from "here"?* Whether these inquiries are the primary reasons for having a life guidance reading, an akashic or astrological session, or spirit world communication, these are the questions that people most want answers to. From my experience, it is what many *long* to know.

Many people believe that their life purpose points to a specific career choice. Others think it involves being a mother, father, or grandparent. Still others pessimistically fathom that life is about being on the losing end of just about everything. Some hold the position that there is no purpose to life at all — that it's simply a random biological event. During the past several years (and more than ever before), I've observed apathy, anger, depression, confusion, and meaninglessness when it comes to people's understanding of life. I believe that these adverse emotional and mental states result, in great part, from an ongoing collective consciousness revolution that escalated during the coronavirus pandemic in 2020 and continues today.

Since revolution often involves metamorphosis and transformation, what exactly is changing amidst the current turmoil? From my observations, a greater percentage of the population is contemplating the meaning of life, their purposes within it, and how to connect with that purpose. Many do not know how to tune into their soul's voice through intuition. Despite the recent turmoil (or perhaps because of it), humankind is awakening to the truth of our underlying unity aside from external differences. Due to technology, we are no longer isolated. With a simple click on the Internet, we become aware of events worldwide. Viewing these through the lens of higher spiritual consciousness, we're seeing that what affects one affects all — animals and the earth included.

In addition, people today hunger for direction on how to cope with current conditions of confusion, turmoil, uncertainty, mistrust, desperation, divisiveness, violence, and chaos. Although these have always existed, the pandemic in 2020 increased their prevalence exponentially. Depression, anxiety, addiction, and suicide are now widespread maladies.

We're in the Midst of Global Transformation

One would have to be living under the proverbial rock to be unaware of the tumultuous state of today's world. Although humankind has historically experienced deeply troubling conditions, I believe that modern technology (TV, Internet, cell phones, online social media, and video platforms) greatly amplifies the spread — and hence, the awareness of information, placing it squarely and consistently before our eyes and ears. We are inundated with massive amounts of data. Although these modern conveniences often provide positive information and ways of communicating (education, research, entertainment, and socialization), it is glaringly apparent that they also function as hotbeds for debilitating, destructive conditions that lead to divisiveness, isolation, anxiety, anger, envy, depression, despair, and fear. What we focus on with regularity becomes embedded in our consciousness, fueling our thoughts, emotions, and actions — either for humanity's good or detriment. How we *use* technology (which, in itself, is neutral, much like money) determines what it is capable of accelerating.

As I write this, it's astonishingly clear that humanity is in the midst of transformation on a global scale. So, the question becomes: How does this relate to the journey of the individual soul? How do we find solutions that will lift us out of the current morass of confusion, division, hatred, and fear? How can we use our newfound awareness in service to others? As evidenced in my practice of mediumship, I believe that more people than ever are seeking guidance about how to cope with life's maladies and find meaningful, personal direction. Above all, the majority seek peace of mind, clear guidance, and spiritual purpose, yet are unsure how to obtain these and sustain them.

So, what is the answer? Transformation has to necessarily be ignited within each person and catch fire to lift the consciousness of others. In 2023, the world population was an estimated 8.1 billion. Each individual is the presence of God on earth.

Everyone is unique, yet all are the same beneath the façades of race, gender, culture, nationality, and religion.

As the English poet John Donne wrote centuries ago, "No man is an island / Entire of itself." Our spiritual identity is the great unifier. Imagine the monumental positive power that humanity would have if this interconnectedness was realized and the illusion of our separateness was banished. To this end, I offer this book as a guide to hearing, listening to, and following the higher consciousness of your soul in order to live fully, ameliorate suffering, give service, and awaken spiritually.

What You Will Learn on These Pages

Part One focuses on the inner world of the timeless, immortal soul and its unwavering, eternal expression of Spirit — a term that I use interchangeably in the text to also refer to the Divine, Creator, Higher Power, and God. Included in this section is a breakdown of the characteristics of the silent language of intuition and how to recognize it apart from the chatter of the rational mind, external events, and the veneer of the personality. This section also sheds light on the foremost factor that discourages people on their journey: fear. I will discuss how to use this emotion advantageously.

Using the simple analogy of a bridge to illustrate the stages of spiritual transformation, Part Two highlights the meaning and value of surrender to the higher consciousness of the soul, its significance in the process of spiritual transformation, and its astonishing power when embraced. I also discuss the common feelings that frequently accompany the process of deep, meaningful change — sometimes referred to as the "dark night." Here you will find suggestions for navigating through times of discouragement, confusion, and uncertainty. Included in this book part is a chapter on natural laws — the Spirit-given, timeless, immutable principles that ensure homeostasis in all of creation. Knowledge of these laws is invaluable because they are guideposts that offer direction in the transformation process.

Part Three offers insights into the astrological birth chart as a useful map of the soul's past, present, and future potential, followed by a chapter on various soul archetypes, or *rays*. I also cover descriptions of the qualities of each soul group and how they manifest in soul consciousness. I offer an exercise to help you gain insight about which soul group(s) you will recognize as uniquely yours. The final chapter provides more useful, practical exercises, along with meditations to heighten your awareness of intuition, transcend fear, trust your soul's guidance, and remain present in the moment.

You have everything you'll need to embark on the journey of your soul because you contain the essence of Spirit within; you merely have to become aware of this eternal presence then choose to release anything that dims or obscures that indestructible Light. You are meant to be here at this transformative time. Your presence on earth is not by coincidence or accident! No one can take your place in the unfolding divine plan.

Our individual soul's earthly journey is relatively simple in its objective: to uncover and discard layers of internalized, accumulated, false beliefs that obscure its radiance. My sincere hope is that you will apply the principles within these pages to your own situation and circumstances, thus making the exciting adventure of your life smoother, less confusing, more fulfilling, and overwhelmingly joyful.

cjo

Part One

Your Inner Landscape

"So, what are you planning on doing with your life?" asks Mark, a family friend, at my college graduation in June 1980. "Have you landed a job in your field?"

Uh-oh! Although it's a perfectly reasonable question to ask, I'm taken aback and don't know how to respond. I feel my face flush with self-consciousness and my palms begin to sweat. The truth is I have no plans, despite earning a degree in English. The Miss America contestant incident from years earlier seems like a pipe dream now. I am too busy partying and worrying about the fragile, up-and-down relationship with my boyfriend to concern myself with practical details of my future.

A meaningful career is not on my list of priorities. I know it *should* be, but it isn't. *Heck, I don't even know who I am! What should I say to Mark? He's going to think I'm a loser if I don't come up with something. Quick! Think of something!* the voice in my head commands. *Tell him you want to go on to earn another degree. That will impress him.*

"Um, I might go to graduate school to get a Master's in English," I stammer. "I may even go on to get a Doctorate so I can teach at a college and ..." my voice trails off as my uneasiness grows.

Seeing Mark's expression after my response makes me even more uncomfortable: his face transforms from a pleasant, expectant smile into dull blankness. *I guess he expected that I'd be starting a new job next Monday morning!* He quickly looks away, excuses himself and saunters into the dining room with the others. I sense that he knows my "plans" were made up on the spot. I've never been an effective liar.

This snippet of my life at age 22 illustrates how directionless and lost I was in those days. Although I made the dean's list consistently in college, I had no clue as to who I was, what my skills entailed, and what to do with my life. I went to college because it was the thing to do, according to my family and societal standards. Flooding my brain with alcohol and marijuana didn't help with my lack of direction. At age 25, I got sober and the fog lifted, yet the magical answer about what path to seek remained elusive.

If I could be granted a wish today, it would be to have had awareness about intuition and spiritual sensitivity in those early years. If I had known that the answer to my life pathway was not "out there" but inside myself, I believe I would have stepped onto it much sooner. I would have avoided falling prey to numerous self-created challenges, troubles, and heartaches if I would have engaged in intuitive practices, such as meditation, mindfulness, and honest self-appraisal. Most of all, my wish is that I would have had someone to talk with who understood these tools and the importance of using them. This being said, my life unfolded the way it did and in the time that it took — every minute leading me to where I am today. For this, I am grateful.

The inspiration for Part One comes from connecting with clients who were confused, fearful, lonely, discouraged, and addicted, just as I was. During these sessions, I've witnessed my old self expressing these very same qualities. The difference is that I am no longer enslaved by them.

In this section, you will find insights about the distinctions between your personality, ego, and soul, how to know the difference between these "voices," and simple steps that you can take to discover the precious treasure of your soul's wisdom within. You will also learn tools to avoid the pitfalls of your mind's monologue — that of anxiety and fear. Significantly, you'll discover the immense value of following the voice of your soul as it's expressed through intuition.

Are you ready to embark on the fruitful, captivating, delicious journey of knowing yourself beyond your mind, personality, and who you believed yourself to be? Let's begin!

1

Liberation: Discovering the Unlimited, Eternal You

Within you is a sanctuary where you can retreat at any time and be yourself.
~ *Hermann Hesse*

"I'm lost as far as what direction to take in life," Willa, 39, laments during a phone session to connect with her mother, who had recently passed after a long illness. After the mediumship communication is complete, we delve into this question about her life following her mom's death.

"I'm not sure how to ask this," she states nervously. "I took care of my mom for many years, and now that she's gone, I have no idea what to do next. Does Spirit have anything to say about *my* life?"

Willa's situation is one that I've encountered frequently through decades of giving mediumship and life guidance readings. A person's life is consumed with caretaking a family member, and after death occurs, the caretaker's existence feels empty, directionless and, at times, meaningless. People don't know where to turn, how to fill the once-busy hours or who they are apart from their former caregiver role. Just as the soul of the loved one transitions from the physical world into the spirit realm, family members and friends left behind must also make a transition due to that person's absence. It's frequently a time of confusion, disorientation, and adjustment.

"What did you put aside in your life to care for your mom?" I ask.

Willa pauses for a moment. "Well, I can't remember. It's been so long." She's momentarily silent before responding further. "I loved to restore old furniture but I haven't done that in years. I like to remake an old piece and give it a new look. I've worked on bedroom dressers, tables, and lamps. The time used to fly by when I worked on these restoration projects. Is that what I'm supposed to do again?"

"If that is what brought you joy then that is your purpose, or part of it," I respond. "There is no 'supposed to' when it comes to purpose. There are pathways we're drawn to, all of which serve our growth. Creativity is a vital expression of your soul. It's as important to your well-being as caretaking your mom has been. You see, your soul has many facets. It desires to express itself freely in various ways."

"Um, I'll consider that ... but I don't know if I can ..." Willa's voice trails off before she adds, "I might feel guilty doing the restoration work so soon after my mom's death. You know, I think I should be grieving instead of ... well, engaging in a hobby."

"Why? Do you believe your mom wants you to neglect doing something you enjoy? Knowing her love for you, do you think she wants you to be stuck in grief and not go on living? Do you believe she would want that for you? Don't buy into the false belief that the amount of time you spend grieving equals the amount of love you have for someone. That's simply not true. In fact, in many readings I've done, those in spirit encourage their loved ones on earth to engage in life again."

"Okay. I'll give it a try. I know I have to do *something*. Why shouldn't it be something I enjoy? I've felt so empty since Mom passed. Maybe this will help."

By the conclusion of the session, Willa's mood has shifted considerably from grief and uncertainty to hope regarding her new pathway. I have witnessed this very same shift thousands of times throughout the years during client sessions. This transformation in vision comes from the guidance provided by spirit world communication and the uplifting inspiration that flows from the client's own soul.

Soul, Personality, and Ego

Throughout past centuries, there have been countless discussions and writings by theologians, religions, various sects, and spiritual organizations about what constitutes the human soul. Although debates and disagreements abound about the specific nature of the soul's journey, its purpose in our earthly life, what happens upon death, and the subject of reincarnation, the majority of these discussions agree on what comprises the *soul*. It is created by the Divine in its likeness and, as such, is inseparable from its Creator because it contains the very essence, imprint, and template of that Creator. The illusion of separateness from the Divine — as we experience in the physical world — is what we must overcome in order to feel the soul. Living in a world of seeming duality, it's difficult to conceive of unity with God and others. We must realize that our soul consistently speaks to us through the voice of intuition. That voice never leads us astray, even if we don't understand it at times.

During years of practicing mediumship with people from all walks of life, I have personally observed substantiating evidence of the soul's divine characteristics of permanence, unlimited potential, and intrinsic intelligence. If there is a singular tenet of which genuine mediumship gives proof, it's the indelible, eternal, elevated consciousness of a soul during and after physical life. This principle alone is fundamental in helping people realize that their loved ones in spirit go on and remain bonded to them through love.

Additionally, mediumship gives immeasurable comfort for people to know that physical life and death are natural cycles of their souls' journeys. Often, this healing benefit of mediumship is overlooked, although it is just as important as contact with loved ones in spirit through the evidence and messages presented. The phenomenon of communication with souls in nonphysical dimensions is a compelling demonstration of their active, ongoing intelligence and continued awareness beyond the death of the physical body. Our earthly life is a single grain of sand on the beach of eternity. Whether we are clothed in a body or existing in the spirit world as a pure soul, consciousness remains.

Simply stated, the soul is Spirit, or God consciousness, that has taken individuated form. The soul is the imperishable life stream of God that animates each life form on the planet. Because the natural state of a soul is union with the Creator, souls intuitively seek reunion with the Creator from their individuated form via the evolution of their consciousness throughout multiple lifetimes.

From this perspective, all souls share a unified intent: to reunite with their Creator through purifying their consciousness of all that is not in alignment with the Creator. While this is the common purpose that all souls have, each life is unique in its evolutionary stage. That purpose can be and is expressed in countless ways through each individual. This is the meaning behind the expression, "All pathways lead home." No life is superior to another; each soul is precious and irreplaceable in the totality of Spirit. The unfolding of each soul's life experiences offers multiple opportunities to progress spiritually toward its final destination of reunion with the Divine. Many of these earthly experiences are heartbreaking, devastating, and painful; others are pleasant, jubilant, and overwhelmingly joyful. The entire spectrum of human experience and emotion gives souls the chance to recognize and embrace the presence of Spirit within.

Perhaps the best way to further define the soul is to understand what it is not: the body, gender, race, culture, nationality, the mind, beliefs, the personality, and thoughts. Most of humankind's problems originate from identification with these outer characteristics that are used by the soul to evolve spiritually. This is precisely the reason why it is damaging (in terms of spiritual awareness) to believe that we are our body, gender, race, nationality, or any other external condition. Identifying with these outer conditions actually obscures the realization of the underlying unity with other humans and animals. Until we learn this fundamental, inescapable truth, we will continue to sow seeds of division, misunderstanding, violence, prejudice, and hatred. In addition to reunion with the Creator, the realization of unity with all of life is another primary, essential lesson in the schoolroom of earth.

In past writings, I've delved into the distinct conditions that the physical plane offers to souls in terms of evolution, and so I will merely mention here that this world is the perfect environment of contrast (duality) within which the body, the personality, the ego/mind, and myriad personal limitations exist in order for souls to grow. In fact, these characteristics are chosen by the soul before birth to serve its need to spiritually evolve *beyond* them. We come into physicality to learn who we are *not*, and through that process, we remember who we *are* as divine beings. For more on the soul's sojourn in the physical and spirit worlds, refer to my book, *Soul to Soul Connections: Comforting Messages from the Spirit World*.

It's important to realize that the soul's perspective differs significantly from the personality's, which is closely related to the ego. Simply put, the *personality* is a set of qualities that makes each person distinct from another. Examples of this would be the characteristics we use to describe another, such as "fun-loving," "arrogant," "reserved," "friendly," "selfish," or "outgoing." We can think of the personality as a demeanor that is typically apparent to others, or qualities that we consistently embrace and express.

9

The *ego* is a complex of ideas, beliefs, defense mechanisms, conditioned responses, emotional patterns, and recurring thoughts that center on the self, the "I." Its primary functions are to protect itself (and the individual) from vulnerability, harm, and dissolution. The ego's greatest fear is its own death. As we will discuss later, identification with the ego can lead to a multitude of problems, such as self-doubt, fear, anxiety, narcissism, depression, internal criticism, and self-righteousness, among others.

The ego has no awareness of the soul's unity with others because it perceives reality from the distorted vision of separateness. It sees itself as being in competition with others, is relatively self-absorbed, feels superior (at times) to others, and exists apart from God. It recognizes goal-based achievements as being vital to its well-being and success.

When these self-perceptions become exaggerated, excessive or denied, the ego strives for "more" from the external world to fortify itself. Thus, it creates a never-ending cycle of seeking authentic power, peace, and purpose where they will never be found: in relationships, money, possessions, a career, sex, substances, and rational knowledge. The ego's perception of life is one of continually seeking, but never finding. Often, this relentless pursuit continues until one inevitably crashes through catastrophe in some form.

I've seen many illustrations of the stark differences between the perspectives of the ego and the soul during readings, particularly when there are unresolved emotional issues between clients and their loved ones. Although the soul chooses its personality before birth to advance itself spiritually, the personality dissolves upon death because it is no longer useful in the spirit world. I have had to explain this to people when their loved ones in spirit communicate messages seemingly out of character for them.

Consider this example from a client session: Steven receives evidentiary messages from his late father, though he later reveals to me that his intent prior to the reading was to hear from his mother in spirit. (This session is also a good example of the spirit world being in control in sessions, and not me as the medium.) Among the messages in the hour-long session is one that perplexes Steven; in fact, it confuses and upsets him so much that we spend the remainder of our allotted time together discussing it.

"Your dad says he's truly sorry for how he treated you during life," I relay to Steven. "He was very critical, harsh, and demanding of you. He says he imposed his expectations on you and asks for your forgiveness. I'm seeing the symbol of a bended knee, which means a sincere, humble apology from the spirit communicator. Your dad regrets acting as he did during life."

There's silence on the other end of the phone. Then, "I don't want to hear from him!" Steven exclaims. "And I don't believe he would say something like that! My father had no time for me when he was alive and now he wants to apologize? He put his work first, drank heavily, and constantly made excuses for his behavior. That [what I relayed] doesn't sound like him. I've always felt as if I let him down. He never told me he loved me," Steven says, choking up.

"Yes, that was his personality: harsh, demeaning, and critical. He had a strong ego. But he is now aware from his soul's perspective that he hurt you and others, and that this must be acknowledged for these wounds to heal. It was not possible for him to admit this since his earthly personality was so overbearing and he was in denial of his behavior. But his current soul consciousness knows the damage he did. You might consider this before dismissing the message. This is not to excuse his treatment of you, but to shed light on it. Think about how this relationship, as painful as it was, helped you to become who you are today. Your father was a teacher for you; a 'shadow' one, for sure, but still a teacher. What have you learned about yourself through this relationship?" I ask.

"Well, I suppose I've learned self-respect and self-worth since he never gave me those. As years went by, I realized I'd have to find that for myself. It hasn't been easy. I felt like a failure for years because of him. Relationships have been tough for me. But since he's died, I've spent time thinking about all those years I felt useless and unworthy. I realized that I wasted time believing those negative self-concepts. I made a decision to change and grow, despite his negative treatment of me."

"Then you've learned what you needed to from him," I explain. "As tough as it was, you've passed the test."

At the conclusion of the session, Steven admits that he's felt burdened by carrying his painful past with his father, and that he would ponder the messages given during the reading. It was clear that he needed to further purge himself from these internalized self-depreciating messages. I haven't heard back from Steven, but a seed for letting go of the past was undeniably planted during our time together. Hopefully, it will bloom brightly and beautifully.

I cannot stress enough that we are not our rational mind, personality, or ego! Their primary value in terms of spiritual growth is to be servants of the soul's intent, to advance its purpose of alignment and reunion with the Divine. So many times, we attempt to invert this fact by placing them above our true identity as Spirit. Invariably, this approach fails since the mind, ego, and personality are finite and ephemeral compared to the permanence of the soul.

The results of giving them undue importance can be devastating. Most of us have witnessed people living through the dictates of their ego as they fall from grace, or crash and burn. This does not mean the personality is bad or wrong; but to live harmoniously and successfully, the ego, personality, and soul must be in balance, with the soul taking the lead where motivation and intent are involved. If we follow the passion of our hearts and consider how our lives can benefit others in altruistic service, we are in sync with the soul's perspective. Remembering this will reduce unnecessary suffering, conflict, problems, and confusion in life.

Outer and Inner Landscapes

From the time we are born, we are inundated with information: ideas, behaviors, emotions, images, and thoughts from the environment, family, friends, community, schools, the medical field, culture, and religion. These entities are what I call the *outer landscape* since they are external to us. Another term for these is "consensus reality" since they are formulated by collective (mass) thinking and agreement among groups of people. While these externalities offer support, service, education, stability, and nurturing, they are also sources of our deeply ingrained beliefs.

What *are beliefs*? They are convictions based upon ideas that *are suggested to* be true and are agreed upon by the consensus, even though they may not necessarily be substantiated through direct evidence. Beliefs are neither "right" nor "wrong" but rather opinions of the group-consensus landscape. They vary across cultures, change throughout the generations and are, at times, rigidly held. Many times, we feel an allegiance or adherence to beliefs of a particular group (out of loyalty or fear of being different), even if the intuitive voice of the soul — our *inner landscape* — tells us otherwise. This disharmony of conflicting beliefs amongst groups of people is called *cognitive dissonance*, an uncomfortable, stressful psychological state that ultimately must be resolved in order to restore harmony within the psyche of persons experiencing it.

In 1957, Leon Festinger developed the theory of cognitive dissonance after observing members of a cult who believed the earth would be destroyed by a flood. The most committed members of the cult had previously given up their homes, families, and jobs to work for the cult. When the flood obviously didn't occur, the less devoted cult members realized that they had been wrong in believing this; but the staunchly loyal members believed the earth was saved because of their faithfulness to the cult which, in their estimation, averted the flood.

Festinger postulated that humans have the need to be consistent in all of their attitudes, beliefs, and behaviors. When this does not occur, cognitive dissonance arises.[1] This disharmony produces psychological stress and ultimately must be resolved to reestablish harmony of beliefs. Spiritually speaking, cognitive dissonance occurs when people adhere to the beliefs, structures, and dictates of the outer landscape out of habit, allegiance, guilt, and fear, suppressing and repressing the inner realm of their own souls.

An example of listening to the outer landscape is a person who gets married and has children to adhere to the beliefs of her family, who expects its members to do so, regardless of the individual's personal wishes to remain single and dedicate herself to a career, or innate feeling that motherhood is not her soul's destiny in this lifetime. She may try to convince herself that this choice is fulfilling and "the right one," despite her inner promptings. Eventually, the stress between her soul's desires and the wishes of her family becomes overwhelming, usually resulting in transformation through crisis: a divorce, illness, estrangement from the family, or an emotional or mental breakdown.

Another example is a person who remains in a lucrative or prestigious career that satisfies his or her spouse's desire for material gain, despite being miserable in that career. Feelings of inauthenticity arise in the individual but are ignored, repressed, and extinguished by the pressure of expectations and others' demands. In cases such as this, the stress of cognitive dissonance intensifies until the individual reaches a breaking point and seeks resolution to alleviate the psychological stress.

If we choose to follow others' expectations for our lives, we frequently regret not listening to the soul's voice, especially when we feel the pain of betraying ourselves. At some point in our spiritual growth — through discontent, burnout, boredom, or illness — we can no longer deceive ourselves, and we begin to listen to the voice of the inner landscape. The timing for such an awakening is dependent upon the personal consciousness of the soul, the choices made, and the level of stress held. Since every soul's primary purpose is unification with the Divine, it's inevitable that this breaking away from the outer consensus will occur.

According to Bronnie Ware, author of *The Top Five Regrets of the Dying: A Life Transformed by the Dearly Departing,* the number one regret of people facing death is not having lived a life true to oneself and instead lived according to the expectations of others.[2] Ware's writing is based on her personal experiences of interviewing people whom she'd met while giving them palliative care. These stories offer proof that many people have deep regrets at the end of life about not following their souls' calling.

In contrast to the limited capacity of the rational mind, ego, and personality, the soul's consciousness is spacious, all knowing, and unlimited. This is the inner landscape, which functions independent of time and space. It is always leading us on the journey of spiritual evolution, our birthright. The pot at the end of the rainbow doesn't contain actual gold or fleeting material pleasures, but it does offer contentment, fulfilment, and inner peace. In fact, human beings are hardwired for evolution. Can you envision a world where we do not evolve? What might a reality bereft of change look like? I believe the end result would be stagnation and decay, ultimately leading to devolution of the human species. Adaptation is essential for the survival of any species, yet it is indeed possible for human beings to devolve. The choice is ours. Given the state of today's world, we stand at this critical juncture.

The root of most of our problems lies in allowing the ego-identified self to take precedence over the spirit self. If we'd give as much attention to the inner landscape as we do the outer, many of our problems wouldn't exist. It's as if we have become hypnotized into believing that we *are* these outer selves through the repetition of automatic, ingrained reflexes.

As we know all too well that when our ego is threatened in any way, we react with defensiveness, fear, anger, jealousy, sadness, or hatred. It's important to note that although many New Age teachings demonize the ego and personality as hindrances to spiritual growth, they are necessary for the soul's sojourn in the physical world. If they weren't, we would not have them. The outer landscape provides multiple opportunities for meaningful work, service to others, relationships, communing with nature, and community. Both inner and outer landscapes are needed in the process of transformation; although, ultimately, we must honor the evolutionary intent of our soul's consciousness above all else. Combining the outer landscape with the inner is key to progressing in the incredible journey of life.

Many of the problems we create can be boiled down to the singular truth that we often have no idea who we really are beyond the beliefs and dictates of family, culture, education, religion, media, and government. In other words, we give too much weight to the outer landscape, often at the expense of our inner promptings. And although these social constructs are valuable in their own right, they are manifestations of outer consensus reality, and thereby concerned with the physical world. As long as we see them for what they are — human constructs and not the reality of who we are — we are far less prone to becoming enslaved by them at the expense of our true inner identity. As stated earlier, it's true that there is much value in the outer landscape; through it, the soul can experience contrast, duality, and karma (cause and effect) to serve its growth. Although these conditions of the outer landscape are essential, it's important to not allow them to define us since they are not the ultimate goal of our existence.

What Is Spiritual Evolution?

If our sole purpose for coming to the physical plane is to remove layers of false beliefs that obscure the soul's light, why do we take on these layers to begin with? Allow me to explain. We create them through our identification with and attachment to our thoughts, emotions, and actions in response to life experiences during both past and present journeys on the physical plane. Because we've created them, we are directly responsible for them. (This is due to the Law of Cause and Effect. For more on this, see Chapter Six on natural laws.) They can only be removed by becoming aware of our soul's desire and will to express itself more purely.

No one can make us change; that incentive must come from within. That being said, we own the gifts of choice and free will. These are our birthright, given to us by Spirit. The closer we align our choices with our soul's intent (which, in turn, is in alignment with Spirit), the easier our life flows. The advice to "go with the flow" applies here. So, while we do indeed have free will, we can save ourselves from regret by making choices that align with the divine pathway of the soul. To help you discern the difference between your personal will and the divine will (of your soul), I've listed qualities of both in the next chapter.

While there are ongoing discussions within metaphysical and spiritual communities as to whether human beings actually do have choice or free will, my experience in giving thousands of readings points to the reality of free will. Debates about its existence range from the belief that we are destined for certain circumstances over which we have no control to those that maintain there is no greater (supreme) power than our personality, ego, emotions, and desires. While there is value in examining all of these thoughts, the fundamental, immutable truth is that each of us is accountable for the choices we make because of the existence of natural laws. As you will see in Chapter Six, these eternal laws always supersede man-made laws, despite one's possible ignorance of them.

When most people ask about their life purpose, they are really asking about the choices in life that will fulfill them in a deep, meaningful way. The answer to this is not complex. Contemplate which choices align with your soul's intent in its path of growth. Which outcome brings you closer to your true identity? What takes you away from it? In most cases, the correct choice has little to do with the outer landscape, such as money, others' approval, religious dogma, cultural dictates, or societal expectations.

There are numerous examples in the readings I've given from souls in the spirit world who communicate messages about their choices and the repercussions of them. These messages involve apologies for mistreatment of others (as shown in the story of Steven's father), regret for succumbing to addictions, unbalanced emotions, and prioritizing money and work over relationships and genuine inner happiness. These souls mention that they've become aware of the repercussions of their choices during the life review process (a spiritual assessment) that occurs shortly after death. Some souls admit to knowing that they should have chosen differently during their earthly life, but did not. A compelling portion of the life review is the firsthand experience of how one's choices affected others and how others felt as a result of them. If hindsight is 20/20, this life review in the spirit world provides perfect, unfiltered vision! But we do not have to wait until we die to have these revelations. They're available to us now by going within and taking an honest self-assessment.

In contrast to messages of regret are the communications from those in the spirit world that affirm good choices made during their physical lives. Below is a brief excerpt from a reading in which Catherine's son, Michael, (who passed in a car accident) imparts messages about his kindness to others throughout his life.

After giving several pieces of evidence about his life and death, Michael impresses me with how he treated others during his life. I pass this along to Catherine.

"I tried to help others as much as I could. I wanted to be a friend to those in need. I know you didn't always understand this, but it was important to me. Now I see that doing so was a worthwhile choice when I reviewed my life here, Mom."

"Yes, he was a friend to many," Catherine responds with tears. "I worried about him because he talked to strangers all the time. Several times, he invited homeless people to stay with him in his apartment. I don't know how he had that level of trust, but he did. He never met anyone he didn't like and reached out to many who felt lost."

Michael then explains that he is doing the very same thing in the spirit world. "Mom, I'm helping newly crossed spirits find their way here. I am what is called a 'greeter' and I assist those who are disoriented and afraid at death to feel at home here. I got this 'job' because I helped people in this way during my earthly life. I earned it. I am okay and at peace."

In the spirit world, where personality and ego do not exist, there is a knowing that all choices should lead to the nourishment of the soul, giving to others and having benevolence for all beings as Spirit. Thus, if we strive for the highest in our lives, we will elevate our consciousness both here and in the afterlife.

Can we evolve spiritually or find purpose without practicing a religion? While all religions serve a purpose in spiritual evolution, our consciousness can and does expand beyond the established dogma of theology. At their core, all religions contain the kernel of truth that there is a higher consciousness (whatever they may call it) beyond the boundaries of our finite physical self and rational mind. All teachings emphasize the importance of love, forgiveness, and ongoing communion with the Divine through prayer and service to others. Coupled with this is the belief that there is a force greater than ourselves that we can connect to when healing is required, a power that is available to everyone equally. While all of these tenets of major religions are valid, we do not have to be religious to experience them, for we have the light of Spirit within, which is accessible to us at all times. By practicing stillness and meditation, you can easily experience higher consciousness through your own desire to merge with it.

The Role of Spiritual Teachers in Self-Discovery

Because I have had many years of training in mediumship, spiritual healing, astrology, and spiritual development, I have studied with many different teachers and read countless books on these topics. From these experiences, I've come to recognize that authentic spiritual teachers possess specific qualities that set them apart from ego-driven ones. I share these here in order to help you discern legitimate teachers from those who are not.

Throughout time, people have followed spiritual teachers and gurus to obtain spiritual wisdom to improve their lives through the application of principles associated with a spirit-centered life. Many of these teachers were wise, humble, intuitive, ethical, practiced in spirituality, and genuinely concerned with helping others. For example, Jesus, the Buddha, and Paramahansa Yogananda were dedicated spiritual masters whose core teachings focus on dedication to Spirit, love, forgiveness, and service. Their teachings have transformed millions by imparting timeless truths of genuine spiritual consciousness and demonstrating the way to a righteous path of living from one's heart. Studying these timeless spiritual teachings is uplifting, inspiring, and life-transforming.

A true, genuine teacher wants nothing but independence, wisdom, and spiritual growth for students. Most good teachers readily admit that they learn just as much from their students as the students absorb from them. A pure spiritual teacher combines knowledge and compassion in service to others. The main objective of bona fide teachers is the transmission of timeless wisdom, based on natural laws. They teach from the perspective of universal truth, not from a personal agenda.

On the other hand, there are false teachers who are not reputable, are ego-driven, self-righteous, narcissistic, and materially oriented. Some lead cults in which followers are compelled to give complete allegiance and money to the leaders. Unfortunately, many well-meaning, unsuspecting, vulnerable people are deceived by those who put up a convincing, rosy, charismatic front that obscures their real intent of wielding control over others, fostering dependency, demanding large sums of money for their teachings, and ostracizing or condemning those who dare to question their teachings or walk away from them.

People who feel directionless, isolated, confused, and lost in life are especially vulnerable when it comes to these unethical teachers. Examples of false, dangerous, manipulative "teachers" in recent history are Jim Jones, who led the Peoples Temple, Bonnie Nettles and Marshall Applewhite (Heaven's Gate cult), and more recently, Keith Raniere of the NXIVM cult based in New York. All presented themselves as having "special" secret knowledge that would lead to the personal and/or spiritual redemption of their members. They promised extraordinary spiritual enlightenment, sanctuary from impending doom, advanced personal development training and, in the case of NXIVM, material wealth.

The best defense against falling prey to such teachers is to be aware that they exist and to use wise discernment regarding character. To do so, it's crucial to research the teacher, their curriculum, the values they espouse, and testimonials from current and former students. A genuine teacher will never encourage dependency, insist on a student's complete allegiance, or demand exorbitant fees for services. Your intuition will steer you to the teacher who is best suited to your needs. Trust it.

It's important to consider that while many teachers are concerned with their students' well-being, we all must also do the necessary inner work alone. No one can give us spiritual self-realization. The best teachers point students in the direction of the inner pathway of the soul. They model what they teach and "walk" the teachings they impart. Genuine teachers realize that they are only channels for the information presented, not the source of it. Their role is to stoke the fire of Spirit within students and leave the rest to students themselves. The teacher plants seeds, which students must subsequently nurture through dedicated self-discovery, practice, and service.

Relax and Be Patient with the Process

Nearly 30 years ago, I stepped onto the path of spiritual development. When I recall those early days, various experiences come to mind. From the first day that I entered the quaint metaphysical center in my hometown, I felt like I had come home. The center offered spiritual healing and reiki training, psychic development instruction, and a variety of workshops, including natural healing remedies, sacred geometry, spiritual symbols, and meditation. I enthusiastically signed up for these and borrowed many books and cassette tapes from the center's library. I recall feeling as if I could not "download" this material quickly enough to satisfy my intense thirst to learn and grow. This stemmed from my passionate intent to know what existed beyond my ordinary consciousness and to discover the unseen, metaphysical world of healing powers, the spirit realms, the akashic files, and the storehouse of the subconscious mind. My intent, desire, and passion to investigate these subjects fueled my own spiritual growth and quest for self-discovery. In fact, these are the very qualities that motivate individuals to want to know their soul's journey. In turn, they accelerate the passage into higher awareness.

Because our soul's single reason for coming into the physical plane is to reunite with the Creator, the intent and desire to do so produces a quickening within our consciousness, although we need to periodically take breaks to integrate each step on the path. If we rush the process to reach a self-imposed goal, we usually end up overwhelmed and burned out. In our zest to learn, we can take on too much at once, leaving little time for the new information to germinate within.

When I look back on those early days in my personal journey, I find it humorous that I mistakenly believed I was done with certain lessons and the next goal needed to be pursued. "Next!" was my personal mantra in those days. I wanted "it" all now. When life presented difficult circumstances that I believed I had already mastered, I felt as though I had failed at applying my newfound inner knowledge. Then I would become discouraged, doubtful, and angry. *But I've already dealt with that! Why isn't this stuff working?* I'd complain. Interestingly, I realized years later that one of my soul's lessons was to learn patience — something I had little of at the time. Once I woke up to this, my life slowly transformed into a much gentler, laid-back approach. By experiencing frustration for years, I learned to not rush, live day by day, and surrender to the moment. As my spiritual guides pointed out to me at the time, unpleasant emotions are wakeup calls that something is out of balance. And, indeed, I was unbalanced.

My advice to you is to slow down, live one day at a time and be patient with the process. Learn to listen intuitively to the voice of your soul. Awakening spiritually is not a race or competition. At times, you will take two steps backwards for one taken forward. Relax. You'll assuredly get there, one day at a time.

Accessing the Pause Between Your Thoughts

Choose a special spot in your home where you'll not be disturbed. Sit quietly with your eyes closed, your spine straight and your hands in your lap.

Focus your awareness on your body, starting with the feet and moving slowly up your body to the top of your head. As you proceed, notice any sensations that arise in each part of the body. Don't judge any of these, simply become aware of them. If your mind wanders, gently pull it back to your body.

When you are finished, open your eyes and note how you feel. Did you notice that when you focused on the various body parts, the stream of your usual, repetitive thoughts slowed? As you placed your attention on sensations, what happened to thoughts generated by your mind? Did they slow or disappear?

You can repeat this exercise using your breath as a focus, with the rise and fall of your chest as the focal point. This exercise will help you to recognize the pause between thoughts where the pure consciousness of your soul is expressed. This is the "you" beyond thoughts and rational mind.

Be assured that all you need to know and trust the journey of your soul is the intent and desire to do so. In the midst of troubling, uncertain circumstances, you can turn to the one sure resource within. This doesn't require money, a special environment, magical tools, excessive amounts of time, or anything else, for that matter. As you will discover along the way, the invaluable excursion into your deepest self is yours for the asking. Are you ready to go?

2

Intuition: The Expression of Your Soul

When you reach the end of what you should know,
you will be at the beginning of what you should
sense.
~ Kahlil Gibran

"I wonder if you can help me understand why I feel unfulfilled in my work in accounting," asks Ashleigh, at the beginning of her session with me. "I make a high salary and I went to college to learn this field, but for the past year or so, I feel drained after coming home from the office. I dread going into work most mornings. I'm just going through the motions. I feel there is something else I need to do. What's going on?"

Her voice is thick with tiredness, resignation, and discouragement. Before responding, I tune into Ashleigh's soul by silently asking, *What is it you want her to know?*

Her soul immediately replies. *Ashleigh believes she is stuck in her career but I tell her she is so much more than her need to earn a living! I give her promptings to let herself dream about the things that make her feel alive, bring her joy, and feel connected to others, but she dismisses my guidance as frivolous nonsense and untrustworthy. She believes she has to keep doing this job because of the income it provides and the time invested. She neglects the advice I give her by saying she doesn't have time to do much except work. I've also told her this job is no longer meeting her needs for fulfillment. Perhaps you can get through to her. This is why she scheduled a session with you.*

From this soul-centered message, I know she is burned out and exhausted from working at a job that her heart is not in. Her soul desires and begs for nourishment. Going deeper into her emotions and physical body, I perceive restlessness, boredom, fatigue, and stress in her neck and shoulders.

"Your soul is speaking to you through your intuition, emotions, and body that you need something beyond what you're currently doing. I sense you long to go deeper, to have contact with people, not numbers. There's little passion for this current job. An enhanced connection is something your soul longs for. Do you agree?"

"Yes, I do, but I can't just quit without another option!" Ashleigh responds impatiently. "I'm interested in learning holistic healing practices but I don't see how I can make a living from that. There's a group of people in my area who practice energy healing. They invited me to join them, so I signed up for a course in that. Should I still do it?" she inquires. "I mean ... well, if I can't earn a living from it, is it worthwhile for me to learn?"

"You may not make a living from energy healing but money is not the be-all or end-all when it comes to your soul's fulfillment. Your soul desires to serve God. Take the class with no goal in mind, no expectations, except to try something new and interesting. At the very least, this will give your soul the nourishment that you're not receiving through paid work," I suggest. "And when you feel bored or drained at work, allow yourself to feel the excitement of learning something new in your off time. This will feed your innermost being and give you something to look forward to. Think about how this workshop can benefit your soul, not your income."

At the conclusion of the session, Ashleigh agrees to take the energy healing class without expectations. She promises to let me know how this new endeavor goes.

Six months later, Ashleigh contacts me for another session. As soon as I hear her voice, I sense a profound difference in her disposition. She sounds clear, vibrant, and strong, a remarkable difference from our earlier session.

"I took the first course in healing and am now signed up for the second!" she announces excitedly. "Thank you for encouraging me to do that. I feel much better when I go to work. I look forward to the group healing exchanges. Doing healing work gives me what I was missing: a deeper connection with God and helping others. I feel alive again. I'm also on the lookout for a new job. Most of all, I now feel as if I'm listening to my soul."

Throughout the years, I have encountered numerous clients like Ashleigh who seek validation about what they are already feeling from the depths of their souls. It's much like obtaining a second opinion on a troubling medical condition, although the soul's workings certainly aren't scientifically based. Some are seeking permission to follow those feelings, even though no one needs this to do so. After witnessing countless examples, I'm convinced that we'd all be much happier, contented, and peaceful if we'd give regular, healthy doses of attention to the voice of the soul and its intuitive promptings. We'd *act* from real spiritual awareness instead of *reacting* from ingrained beliefs, rational analyses, and others' dictates. Too often, people do not recognize the inner voice; or they ignore it, or worse, dismiss it. To obtain clarity of inner direction, we must be able to distinguish the difference between the narrative of the mind and the urgings of the soul. Read on to discover some helpful suggestions on how to do this.

The Treadmill of the Mind's Inner Monologue

There's no denying the power of the human mind — its reasoning capability, the ability to perform complex tasks, organize, storehouse millions of facts, formulate language, process information, and retain memories. As research continues to advance in psychology and neuroscience, it reveals previously unknown faculties of the physical brain, how it functions, its structure, and how disease occurs (such as various types of dementia and mental illness).

In addition to scientific research, there is speculation among metaphysicians that the human brain acts as a "step-down" unit for the higher consciousness of the soul. After considering this theory, I agree; however, I sense that the brain receives and interprets only a fraction of the enormous capacity of the soul. This is due to its relatively finite, linear manner of processing incoming information in comparison to the soul's unbounded capacity to do so.

In other words, our brains are able to conceive only bits of our true potential as divine beings, and we are fortunate if we receive even that much. Flashes of insight, answers to seemingly unsolvable problems, and clever inventions are not merely results obtained from the rational mind; they emanate from the higher mind of Spirit, despite our lack of recognition. The timing of these breakthroughs is dependent on the receptivity of our consciousness in any given moment. This fact applies to collective human consciousness as a whole and is why we sometimes hear of stunning advancements in medicine, science, and technology occurring around the same time in different countries and continents. (The isolation and identification of the HIV virus in 1984 by both French and American researchers is an example.)

The quality of the mind that is most relevant to our discussion of intuition is its ability to create a *narrative* — a story based on preconceived beliefs, the past, thoughts, and experiences. This is the well-worn monologue we repeatedly tell ourselves (and others) based on our personal experiences, challenges, family relationships, and assimilation of the prevailing culture's beliefs. Over time, this narrative becomes hardwired into our brains, forming conditioned responses to circumstances in life. This means that our mind *reacts* to stimuli from our environment and others, based on previously conditioned, preformed patterns of thought.

Think of it as a script we follow when we encounter similar or identical circumstances throughout life. This is not necessarily wrong; it is a natural function of the brain for stability, protection, security, and self-preservation. However, when we react to life based solely on the monologue we have created, we limit ourselves to the confines of that narrow box. We feel stuck, bored, overwhelmed, discouraged, hopeless, and tired. These distressing conditions are not necessarily present to lead us down a path of ruin and stagnation; they are signposts to an alternate way of life which is in alignment with the higher consciousness of the soul. "Negative" feelings are red flags that indicate we need to examine and adjust our perspective of life, or something in it.

As conditioned responses repeat and become ingrained over time, they form the structure of our story: who we believe we are, what we believe we are capable of, our perceived strengths and limitations, our talents, value or worthiness as an individual, and many other core self-perceptions. We tend to also view others and the world through the lens of our own story. We believe that we *are* the narrative and that's precisely where troubles originate because it is simply untrue, despite the mind's insistence.

As mentioned earlier, we form defense mechanisms (denial, anger, jealousy, hatred, shame, and sadness, for example) to protect ourselves from perceived threats to the self-created narrative in our minds. Understanding that these reactions occur is the first step in recognizing the narrative when it arises because nothing can be transformed until we become aware of its existence. Unfortunately, many people are not aware of their repetitive thoughts because they deeply identify with them and believe they are reality.

Indeed, this is the ego's reality, but it's not the soul's. I call this phenomenon "the treadmill of the mind" because the thoughts comprising the narrative travel in a circular manner, gain momentum the longer they are energized through repetition, and ultimately arrive nowhere but the same "destination" we currently occupy in terms of consciousness. We expend tremendous energy to keep the narrative going in order to protect ourselves, thus maintaining a level of comfort in the familiar. We identify with the narrative and rarely, if ever, question its validity until we are forced to — usually through some form of crisis. After all, the story is who we are, isn't it?

The Treasure Revealed by Cracking the Illusion

In prior books, I've written about *wakeup calls* as they pertain to spiritual awakening through adversity. To offer a brief synopsis here, wakeup calls are life-transforming events and crises that shatter the mind's narrative, potentially giving us the opportunity to discover who we are beyond the inner monologue. They almost always involve emotional, mental or physical suffering, and dissatisfaction with life. Wakeup calls can originate organically through our own awareness (intrinsic) or they can come from the external world (extrinsic). They are valuable to our spiritual evolution because they invoke change. If it weren't for these, we'd become stagnant because we are creatures of habit. Who hasn't experienced some measure of suffering, dissatisfaction, or lack of fulfillment in life? It is a universal human condition.

Examples of extrinsic wakeup calls are natural disasters, accidents, job loss, trauma, and abuse. Intrinsic ones are anxiety, depression, illness, boredom, feeling stuck, and lack of fulfillment. In the case of the latter, ignoring messages from our intuition that something is out of balance often leads to a worsening of these conditions. It's also possible for this to occur with external crises when we don't listen to the inner voice of the soul.

For instance, I've known people who hated their jobs, felt they needed a change, and complained endlessly, but stubbornly persisted in that work until they were eventually fired, seemingly out of the blue. Another example is people who continually experience tension, stress, and unease in a relationship yet ignore and bury these feelings to keep the peace, only to have the relationship eventually erupt and dissolve. One of the 12-step recovery program's mottos states, "It (recovery) was God doing for me what I could not do for myself." The infinite intelligence of our soul hears and responds to our every thought and continually seeks harmony. In the process of spiritual evolution, if we don't listen to inner guidance, Spirit forces our hand through external crisis. Attentive listening to the voice of the soul is all that is required to follow it, if we choose that route. This inner voice is our direct connection to higher awareness, fulfillment, and inner peace.

Major religions speak about the soul's abiding presence. In the New Testament, Jesus responded to the Pharisees' questions about when and where the kingdom of heaven would arrive on earth by stating, "… nor will they say, 'See here!' or 'See there!' For indeed, the kingdom of God is within you." (New King James Version, Luke 17:21.) This scripture demonstrates that God does not "live" in the external world of materiality, but is present within each person; divine consciousness is not something that will come in the future, but is available right now to everyone. The fundamental Christian belief of surrendering to the soul's eternal relationship with the indwelling Christ consciousness is described as being "born again." For this to occur, the ego's grip must be lessened and eventually extinguished.

In Buddhism, the first of the Four Noble Truths regarding spiritual awakening and the dissolution of the ego is that (paraphrased) "There is suffering, unhappiness, and lack of fulfillment." (In Pali and Sanskrit, this is called *dukkha*.) The Second Noble Truth states that the primary cause of unhappiness is attachment to worldly desires, fleeting pleasures, and empty ambitions. These are all impermanent, destined to pass away, and incapable of satisfying the hunger of the soul.

In our efforts to obtain fulfillment, we chase these things and may attain them for a short time, only to re-experience the longing for fulfillment because they do not satisfy the needs of the soul. Much like eating junk food instead of nourishing whole foods when we're hungry, we remain dissatisfied and hungry by chasing fleeting pleasures. This is an addiction to false pleasure. It is only through sensing the deeper truths of life that real fulfillment is born. In Buddhism, for example, true enlightenment of the soul comes from following the Eight-Fold Path as described by the Buddha. (Visit tricycle.org for further study.)

When we experience wakeup calls, we often do not recognize the invitation to go deeper to listen to the soul and discover the spiritual purpose of what the event has to offer. It takes courage, patience, time, and introspection to grasp the life-transforming significance of such events. Difficulties are windows of opportunity through which we may observe and embrace the vastness of our true being, if we allow them. Of course, it is our decision as to which perspective we want to engage: the story created by our mind or the unbounded wisdom emanating from the soul.

Utilizing Traumatic Events for Spiritual Awakening

In my practice of mediumship, I've spoken with numerous people who have successfully used traumatic events in their lives to grow spiritually. These include individuals who have lost children, endured life-threatening illnesses, had addictions, experienced long-term job loss, suffered devastating financial conditions, survived natural disasters, and struggled with painful family estrangements. Each of these dire events cracked people's lives open through various forms of suffering, but also offered them opportunities to transcend the pain through connection with a consciousness higher than the mind, ego, and thoughts. The fact is that most of our spiritual growth happens in the wake of unpleasant events, and not when things are going smoothly; thus, the meaning of the axiom, "No pain, no gain." This doesn't *have* to be the way we awaken, yet it frequently is. The choice to use these events for spiritual awakening is always present.

Being cracked open is a pivotal moment when we are given the chance to examine and change our inner monologue through the higher guidance of the soul. This is accomplished through surrendering oneself to that guidance in trust. The soul sees beyond the mind narrative and knows our potential. (Part Two of this book is dedicated to the indispensable act of surrender during difficult times since it is central to the alleviation of hardships and personal evolution.)

In recent times, humanity was collectively cracked open by the 2020 pandemic. Fear, panic, distrust, insecurity, confusion, sadness, uncertainty, and anger proliferated as people scrambled to "protect" themselves through social distancing, cope with the illness in themselves or help loved ones through it, research information about effective treatments, and obtain vaccines. Controversy persists about the death count from the virus, the validity of advice given by government officials, and the efficacy of the vaccines, yet we witnessed firsthand how it's possible to manage such an event through cooperation, care, and empathy if we don't succumb to fear. Millions of lives were irrevocably altered by this health crisis, and the world is not the same as before.

Despite differing opinions on the outcome, one thing is certain: the stage was well set for human evolution in 2020, although I believe we will not know the true extent of this transformation until years from now. This crisis clearly demonstrates how fear, anxiety, and panic multiply exponentially through external events that exist beyond our control. What we need to learn from these discomforting states is how to effectively cope with them by turning inward to the guidance of the soul, although we may not comprehend this in the midst of turmoil. It is not easy to see how and why traumatic events occur. Life as we know it may be upended or shattered, but the opportunity to reinvent ourselves is always present.

In the last several years, the number of sessions I've done with people seeking life guidance has increased due to the pandemic and the resulting economic downturn, supply-chain shortages, the breakup of marriages, shifts in various industries, forced early retirement, and loss of jobs and businesses. People want to know what direction they should take and how to navigate the "new" reality.

Regarding work, some of these clients were restaurant servers, some desired a job change before the pandemic, others worked in or managed beauty salons, and a few owned businesses that did not survive the widespread shutdowns that occurred. The souls in spirit who help me with my work (my spirit team) have impressed me to impart these uplifting messages during these types of sessions:

- *Your worth is not defined by a job; you have unlimited capacity for adaptation.*
- *Job loss is an opportunity to explore other facets of yourself. You possess other skills that are useful and employable.*
- *You have the freedom to steer your life course because you are the captain of the ship.*
- And significantly: *A job is not your real source of support; Spirit is.*

During life guidance sessions, my spirit team has also encouraged my clients to allow themselves the luxury of dreaming, to imagine what they would do if earning a living was not part of the picture. Why would they suggest this? Typically, people perceive limitations and set ideas about what they are genuinely capable of, due to their restrictive mind narrative. In the free-floating state of imagination where limits are not imposed, endless possibilities exist. This is the domain of the soul, untethered by beliefs, expectations, and rigid scripts. The state of imagination transcends the conditioned mind and reveals unlimited potential.

Concerning some of my clients' inquiries about employment, my team further suggested that they write down what they envision doing, the details of this activity, a scenario of it in their mind's eye and, importantly, imbue the visions with potent emotions such as deep fulfillment, happiness, service to others, contentment, and peacefulness.

The guides also reminded people that what they focus on with passion becomes energized and brought into manifestation as time elapses, due to the natural law of cause (thought) and effect (manifestation). What we focus on expands and strengthens, much like working a muscle of the body. These imaginative wanderings are a playtime where we can think, do, and be anything we desire. The guides have also advised people to not judge what they experience in this space of imagination, and just allow the images and feelings to freely flow. Even though results may not be immediately visible, they urged people to stay the course and develop trust in the guidance of the soul and Spirit.

Your Life Vision

What do you envision for your life? Following the above instructions, what do you see yourself doing, having, or being? How does this feel?

Remember to remove judgment from this experience and focus on your desires with deep feelings which fuel them.

The Goldmine of Intuition

How is imagination related to intuition? It originates from the same place within our brain: the right hemisphere. In addition to having control over the left side of the body, this part of the brain processes emotions, creativity, and insights (seeing and understanding various facets of situations, ideas, and problems beyond the obvious, linear, and rational). In this state of consciousness, there are no rigid rules or judgments; it is free from linear thinking because the boundaries of rationality and logic do not exist.

Interestingly, the ability to communicate with the spirit world is also a function of the right brain. In mediumship training I've taken, one of my teachers emphasized the necessity of exercising the imagination by closing our eyes and navigating internally through a room in our home. We were encouraged to feel the soft, clean sheets of our bed, see the colors on the walls, feel the weight of objects in the space, and imbibe its overall ambiance. Although these sensations may appear to come from memory, it employs the same focus used in developing *clairsentience* (sensing) and *clairvoyance* (seeing).

In workshop trainings for intuition development, I offer an exercise designed to enliven students' imagination by similarly leading them into an imaginary private room. Some have relayed astonishing, detailed accounts of these rooms — their contents, colors, and overall ambiance. Others have mentioned that they met both members of their spirit team and deceased family members in the room. In this state, there are no boundaries of time or space. There is only exploration, sensing, feeling, and observation. Much like exercise invigorates the body, using the imagination heightens and enhances the intuitive consciousness.

Intuition is the space that exists between stimulus (from the external environment) and our response to it. Simply stated, this space is the pure consciousness emanating from the soul without mind-generated thought. It is just as real and palpable as rational thought. The space is not empty as the mind perceives, but abundant with endless potential. Herein lies the goldmine.

Most of us are preoccupied with thoughts of the past or future, which are constructs of the mind. This is one of the reasons why depression (rumination) and anxiety (apprehension) are endemic in our culture. Very few people remember that all we have available is the present moment. Even fewer of us *live* in present time. As one of my favorite spiritual teachers, Eckhart Tolle, points out, we cannot possess the past or future because they exist only as memories and phantoms in our mind. The only available time to any of us (gender, culture, race, or status aside) is the "now" moment. This is the domain of the soul, and where spiritual awareness takes place.

Timelessness is a striking quality of intuition. Have you had the experience of losing track of time when you were engaged in a pleasurable activity, walking in nature, gardening, or visiting a peaceful, lovely place? You may have observed that your attention was immersed in the joy of the activity or place, and not on thinking, analyzing, remembering, or worrying. You were present in the moment, open to the sights, sounds, and sensations of the experience.

Infants, children and animals are experts when it comes to timelessness because they play and experience life apart from the censored lens of the ego and rational mind. This is an unabashed, straightforward, authentic honesty that they naturally radiate. As adults, we have much to learn from these teachers who live in the present moment. This is why I keep an old black-and-white photo of myself at three years old hanging in my room. It reminds me of who I really am at my core. The pure child within is the wisest guide to intuition. I believe this is what Jesus referred to when He said, "Truly I tell you, unless you change and become like little children, you will never enter the kingdom of heaven." (Matthew 18:3.)

Much of the difficulty that people have regarding intuition centers on distinguishing it from personal thoughts. In the early days of my own mediumship training, I, too, struggled with this issue. Today, thousands of readings later, I still occasionally question if my inner perceptions are arising from a different source than my own mind. When this occurs, I do a check-in about the feeling of the perception. For example, does the information feel judgmental, small or fear-based? Does it feel as if it's emanating from outside of me because it is unfamiliar to me? Referring to the list of qualities below will help you gauge your perceptions by sensing the nature of them.

When I teach intuition and mediumship development, people often comment, "I don't know if what I'm sensing is coming from my own thoughts or from my intuition/the spirit world. Maybe I'm making this up." This is a common problem for those in the beginning stages of development, and it's perfectly normal to question the origin of perceptions. Do not be discouraged by this! To help you understand the differences between your thoughts/mind narrative and intuition, here are the significant qualities of each:

- **Mind Narrative:** Self-depreciating, fearful, limiting, repetitious, self-protecting, self-centered, based in the past or future, judgmental, arrogant, angry, victim-identified, doubtful, self-pitying, hopeless, small, and negative.
- **Intuition:** Self-supporting, unafraid, unlimited, fresh (not stagnant), inclusive of others, based in the moment, nonjudgmental, humble, empowering, hopeful, large, positive, and beneficial to humanity, animals, or the planet.

Think of the mind narrative as being on automatic pilot, reacting to life stimuli through conditioned responses, and an inner monologue. Think of intuition as free-flowing, spontaneous, unscripted perceptions. Intuition frequently contains the element of surprise precisely because it is *not* scripted. Unfortunately, many people struggle with this distinction by prioritizing their internal monologue and paying little attention to the relatively expansive perspectives of their souls. This happens for three reasons: First, most people are taught that facts and logic trump feelings and gut sensing. Second, most people fear change and resist the unknown. Last, trust is necessary when following one's intuition, and that takes time and practice. From the time we are young, we're taught that things must be proven or they are not valid. (In Chapter Three, I discuss trust as a vital component of inner knowing.)

In the case of intuition, we cannot rely on external facts to validate what we perceive because they often do not exist at the time when we have the intuitive perceptions. This is the nature of intuition, and precisely why it is often ignored or dismissed. In the case of fear, until it is acknowledged and subsequently transcended, it's nearly impossible to progress by following the soul's promptings. People can remain stuck in this state for years or until death. As with every choice in life, we are responsible for the decision to not evolve. This means that we will face the same or similar circumstances again and again until we master them.

During readings, souls who have chosen to remain stagnant during physical life have imparted to me that they had to confront and work on their previous resistance to spiritual progression once in the spirit world. Growth does not cease with death; it is perpetual until we ultimately reunite with Spirit. My spirit team has conveyed that we short-circuit our growth through our own resistance to it. We must step out of our comfort zone into unknown territory, despite our fears.

No progress in human history has been accomplished without stepping away from the known.

The Three Main Intuitive Senses

Sensing through intuition is called *clairsentience* (from the French, "clear feeling"). This involves perceiving energy from/about people, places, and things without the use of the five physical senses. It's the instinctual feeling we've all had that we can't immediately put our finger on, except to know it's a clear, strong sensation we experience. Often, there is no external evidence to back up our feeling. If you've ever felt uneasy in a particular place, gotten goosebumps during conversations or reading a story (one of the physical signs of energy sensing), felt "butterflies" in your stomach or experienced discomfort around certain people for no obvious reason, you've experienced clairsentience. The same is true when you experience a knowing about people, places, events, and things.

All of us have this inner sense. It's one of the three main intuitive senses we possess; the other two are *clairvoyance* (seeing) and *clairaudience* (listening). These senses have been with us for eons and are hardwired. They serve a vital evolutionary purpose because they offer protection from danger and threats to our well-being by quickly giving us an inside track to appraise the nature of people, places, and things. Are they safe and friendly, or threatening and dangerous, for example? Wild and domesticated animals also have clairsentience as evidenced by their aversion to certain people and other animals, as well as places. Wild animals are known to predict acts of nature before they manifest (tornadoes, earthquakes, and floods, for example) by moving to safe ground before the event occurs.

Clairsentience is received through the energy center that interconnects with the solar plexus (upper and lower abdomen) region of the body; hence, the term "gut feeling." This center is one of the seven major *chakras* (from the Sanskrit, "spinning wheels") through which we assimilate vitality from the environment, the earth, and the Divine. The more open and clear these centers are, the more we are able to sense energy. When engaging in intuitive work, I recommend doing regular tune-ups to your chakra system through meditation, stillness, forgiveness of others, and daily release of lower emotions (anger, fear, jealousy, hatred, control). Keeping your energy field clear greatly strengthens intuition and helps avoid illness through the release of these dense emotions.

Years ago, I attended an intuition workshop at Lilydale, New York, a Spiritualist community. It was being taught by Bear Heart, a Native American shaman and "grandfather" to numerous tribes. An exercise that was particularly intriguing was one in which we wrote a personal question to our soul using our dominant hand. In this dialogue with the soul, we then answered this question by writing the response from our soul with the other hand. Bear Heart's assistant explained that these instructions were meant to engage both sides of our brain in obtaining intuitive insight regarding our questions. Following a brief meditation, we wrote our soul's response to the question using our non-dominant hand. Despite the sloppiness of the handwriting from my left hand (it resembled a child's writing), I was astonished to discover the insights revealed from my soul. Most of them were the opposite of what I'd expected before the exercise. A few were downright shocking! I immediately recognized that the insights were not coming from my rational mind, as they were completely different from my usual mind monologue.

In another exercise in the same workshop, we were led to a quiet wooded area in Lilydale. Next, we were directed to choose a tree to dialogue with, embrace it with our arms, and ask it to communicate wisdom. We were to continue until the flow of information from the tree ceased. No one in the class spoke during this exercise; the rustling of the trees from a light breeze and the birds chirping were the only sounds. There I stood in the silence with my arms around the tall tree, hoping to receive something, anything, and feeling very silly indeed.

Of course, my mind monologue kicked in immediately with ridicule and doubt about the exercise. I silently told it to let go and relax. Soon the feeling of foolishness was replaced with a remarkable flow of communication from the tree: *We (the group of trees in the woods) co-exist here peacefully, even though we are different heights, species, and ages. We stand tall and proud in our own space, without interfering with other trees. We respect one another. We know the entire forest works together as a unit, not as individuals. If only humans would learn from us — to stand tall and honestly, honor one another, and exist peacefully side by side — they could create a much better world. Look to nature, to us, as your teachers.*

When I felt the communication stop, I broke the embrace with the tree and silently thanked it. Walking back to the classroom, a few in the class shared what they had received during the exercise. In all honesty, I believed that I had imagined what the tree had spoken to me, despite the profundity of the communication. Yet the messages were meaningful, sagely, and impactful. More than that, they felt *real* and resonated with my soul. After gauging the event from my soul's perspective, I accepted the validity of the experience. Despite my doubts, I knew it was spiritual truth.

You can tune into your soul's wisdom through becoming still, focusing on your breath, closing your eyes, and asking for its perspective regarding a situation, personal guidance or a confounding problem. Do not judge what you receive. Or choose a peaceful place in nature to commune with this higher consciousness. Write this wisdom in your journal.

Dialogue with Your Soul

Following one of the exercises in the paragraph above, go into a quiet space and dialogue with your soul. It's helpful to write a question before beginning. This can be an inquiry about your life direction, current or past challenges, relationships, or meaningful service.

After a few moments of stillness, write insights you've received from this higher consciousness. Remember, do not judge what you receive; simply write this information down. Become the observer of the writing.

Notice how this guidance is useful to you in the days ahead. What does it reveal?

Animals Are Naturally Intuitive

In addition to taking training in mediumship for human souls, I've also studied animal communication. In multiple readings that I've given, pets of clients come through with those they knew and loved during physical life or with someone the client has asked to take care of them in spirit. Two striking differences between mediumship communication with animals and humans are the former's relative simplicity in the dialogue and the manner in which the information is received. Animals do not have egos as humans do. In this way, they are a pure form of Spirit in their expression and do not engage in duplicity, manipulation, or judgment. They also do not have verbal language as we do so they use pictures to relay their messages during sessions.

From my experience in speaking with them, the style of the communication is straightforward, unembellished, and charmingly childlike. They do not lie or manipulate the dialogue. Besides using instinct for survival, animals are naturally intuitive in that they keenly sense energy of other animals, humans, and the environment. People have often commented to me that they believe their dog or cat is sensing the presence of spirit beings (including deceased pets) in their home. I believe this to be true since animals are naturally very open to nonphysical dimensions.

Cats, especially, are highly sensitive to energy, and it appears that they are naturally intuitive. When I've connected telepathically with my housecats, I've received clear messages from their thoughts. One of these was from Cinders, my small, black, female cat. On this particular occasion, I was on my way into the kitchen and she was on the couch near the entrance to it. When our gazes met, I heard her speak through my intuition: *I want to go into that locked room (the sunroom) to explore the plants in there. I love it in there! It's like being outside. Please let me play in there, near the plants!* She then glanced at the door to the sunroom. I told her (out loud) that she couldn't go in there because she tries to eat the plants which might harm her. A few seconds later, I intuitively sensed her disappointment. Then I felt guilty! I gave her a gentle rub on her head to make her and myself feel better about denying her.

This exercise is especially useful if your pet has behavior issues, conflicts with other pets or if they aren't feeling well. (A visit to the vet is equally important in this case.) You can ask them to tell you what is bothering them, what you can do to make their life better, and anything else you'd like. Make sure you have the pet's full attention before tuning in. This is done through locking gazes or through stroking them. Without thinking, open to sense what your pet communicates to you. You'll be amazed!

By now, I hope you realize the importance of disconnecting from your personal mind when opening a kindred connection with your soul. Fear, doubt, confusion, and insecurity are residents of your ego and rational mind, yet you can and *will* transcend them.

In the next chapter, we will explore these common blocks that arise during times of stress, crisis, and change, as well as how to transcend them through your soul's consciousness, which is eternal, infinite, fearless, and secure. Through it you will know true freedom, compassion, confidence, and invulnerability. Let's continue onto the next leg of our sensing journey.

3

Forging Fearlessly Ahead

Be patient with yourself. Self-growth is tender; it's
holy ground. There's no greater investment.
~ Stephen Covey

"I'm aware of a young man connected to you who passed quickly and unexpectedly. His death feels tragic to me. He shows me my mediumship symbol of self-responsibility regarding his death [his hands pointing towards his chest]," I explain to Michael, who reached out to me for a phone session. "This man stands close to you, indicating a close relationship between the two of you. Does this make sense to you?"

"Um, yes, it does," Michael replies, his voice breaking up. "It's my son, Danny. I can't move beyond his death. It's broken me in pieces. He's the reason I'm having this session."

As my consciousness blends with the young man's, I receive further impressions about his personality, his life, and what emotions he experienced just prior to his passing. "Danny says he was very sensitive and he felt as if he didn't belong here in life. He says he felt that he didn't fit in. He was artistic, and he is showing me his drawings and writings, which you still have. The writing is something he wants to speak of here. He places a red circle around a poem he wrote, one in which he expressed his deepest feelings. He says you've read this and cried."

"Yes, yes, I have that poem right here in front of me!" Michael responds with excitement. "I've read it over and over since he died to try and understand what he was going through. What does he say about it?"

I pause to sense Danny's impressions about this poem. "I'm overwhelmed by feelings of hopelessness, but I keep those to myself. I try to talk about this but I don't even know where to begin. I feel alone, disconnected from others. Writing is an easier way for me to communicate. I put my soul into this poem."

Suddenly, a distinct impression hits me: "Your son's passing was a suicide, wasn't it?" I ask Michael.

"Yes, yes, it was," he says quietly. A moment of stillness ensues.

Next, I feel an overwhelming sense of relief from Danny as he continues impressing me with his story. Then he adds, "One day, I had had enough. That's when I made the decision that I wanted out of this pain. It was a huge burden lifted from me when I decided I'd be better off over here. I didn't realize then how much it would hurt you and Mom. I'm truly sorry. I just wanted out of the emotional pain."

Upon hearing this, Michael blurts out, "I feel so guilty! I should have done more to help him. I feel as if I can't ever forgive myself for not insisting that he get help."

As the reading progresses, I feel that Danny wants to shift the communication away from himself to his dad. "Please, Dad, I want you to know none of this was your fault. I know how horrible you've felt since I left you. I've come to you on your worst days to tell you to live your life again. I've heard you talk to people about how much this hurt you. I'm truly sorry, Dad. You need to find life again. Don't stop living because of me."

Then, another startling, urgent message comes through: "Don't you do it, Dad! I found out over here I made a big mistake by ending my life. It's not the right thing to do!"

I am taken aback by the intensity I feel in this message. This is obviously something he desperately needs to communicate to his dad. There's silence on the other end of the phone. Michael is apparently speechless.

"Michael, are you still there?" I ask, concerned that the call might have dropped.

"Yeah, I am," he finally responds in a barely audible voice. "I don't know how to say this, but since my son's death, I have thought about taking my own life. That's how much losing him has devastated me. I've never told anyone that until right now. So, Danny knows what I've thought! Now I *know* he's around me. This is the first time I've felt a little hope since he died. Truth is, I lost faith in God because of his death."

"He wants you to use his death in a way that will help others," I relay. "He says he's bringing people into your life that you can talk to, people who need to hear his story. Helping them will help you. This will benefit you in moving forward."

At the conclusion of the session, Michael asks me if I could relay a message to Danny. I inform him that he can do this directly, without me. "You have a direct line to your son through the bond of love. If you'd like, you can talk to him right now in this session."

"I just want to tell him that I will not do what he did. I promise to not end my life. I know God is answering my prayer of what to do next with my life, even though I've lost faith."

The session ends with Michael speaking directly to his son: "I love you, Danny! I know you're still with me."

Michael's reading addresses one of the most devastating crises a person can face. His experience of losing a child is one of many I've encountered in my mediumship practice. Facing irrevocable loss leaves parents raw, numb, and devoid of hope and faith. In the thousands of readings I've given that have addressed virtually every possible life situation, the loss of a child is the hardest for people to cope with. That pain is multiplied when suicide is the cause. Like Michael, people often feel crippling guilt on top of other emotions that accompany this traumatic loss. Yet beneath the crushing burden of pain are the ever-present hope, guidance, and healing flowing from the higher consciousness of the soul. No matter what challenging circumstances we face, we must first *trust* that these enduring strengths exist within us. Let's take a closer look at how we can connect with these attributes and use them to move through life's traumas.

Trust Is Essential

Without trust, there can be no awareness of a consciousness higher than our mind. It is vital to our well-being, healing and spiritual growth that we trust in something greater, more powerful and intelligent than our rational mind. As I learned years ago in a 12-step program, this entails relinquishing control of a situation in its entirety to a power greater than oneself. In most 12-step programs, this is called a Higher Power. You can call it whatever you like: God, Spirit, Creator, the Divine, Source. What matters most is that you realize this power is *not* the personal you. It lives above and beyond the personality, mind, and emotions. Your soul is Spirit within — indestructible, eternal consciousness. The act of relinquishing control and letting go may also be called the act of *surrender*, the beginning of your healing, and the very first step in the journey. (In Part Two, I discuss the process and stages of surrender in greater detail.)

For years, I sought answers to situations and events in my life. By way of example, in the early stages of my mediumship career, I was offered several opportunities that promised to increase the number of clients that I would attract. These appeared to be golden tickets that I sincerely believed would expand my work. I was excited and enthusiastic at these prospects. When these did not gel for various reasons, I became discouraged, immensely disappointed, frustrated, and wanted to give up.

Not long after, I sensed a distinct message coming from my soul and spirit team: *Carole, rest in the unknowing.* That was the extent of the message. Initially I was angry. How could I sit back and do little or nothing to make things happen? It didn't make sense. It took time for me to accept what I considered to be a cop-out because of my mind's insistence on controlling nearly everything in my life. Slowly, I let go of *my* way, my perceived need to control events, and began to embrace the concept of trust.

Reflecting back on that time, I now realize that if those opportunities would have panned out, I wouldn't have been prepared to fulfill what they required of me back then. Of course, I could not see that in those days, but each time since then that I've allowed the expanded consciousness of Spirit to guide my life, I've received astonishing opportunities beyond my expectations and far greater than I could have orchestrated on my own. The release of control is one of the most valuable lessons I've obtained, only made possible through my choice to trust.

Trust does not require religious belief; it springs from merely accepting there is divine order and intelligence that emanates from Spirit, *even though we do not understand that* with our rational mind. Developing trust gives assurance that we are not isolated in our perceived hopelessness because the presence of Spirit is all encompassing. Further, this greater intelligence sees a much larger picture of the circumstances that we endure and provides unwavering guidance if we ask for it. It knows what lessons our soul has planned before birth, what will advance our learning, and how to proceed in the face of adversity. In earlier writings, I've referred to this expanded view as the Big Picture, or BP. The human brain, as miraculous as it is, does not comprehend this far-reaching consciousness because it does not lie in the domain of linear thinking. The BP transcends rational thinking, is far-reaching, and is all inclusive.

In whom or what can we place trust outside of Spirit and ourselves, especially these days? Rampant misinformation and deception in the media, government, and online have contributed to generalized distrust today. One day we are told a set of purported facts, and another, we're instructed to disregard those and accept a different narrative. With the invention and proliferation of Artificial Intelligence (AI), it's nearly impossible to know what is real and what is not. Hackers, scammers, impersonators and con artists continually exploit trust by employing increasingly sophisticated means to steal people's data, identity, and finances. Wise discernment is required to avoid becoming a victim of misinformation and thievery. In this digital age, it's little wonder that trust levels are low. This fact is why it's vital to use intuition in the process of discernment. Simply put, if it feels incorrect, wrong, or deceitful, it probably is.

Trust means that even though life does not follow our script or plan, there is another plan — one that we can't currently see — that leads to spiritual evolution and profound healing if we allow it. This leap of faith is not always easy to take, but is essential to the soul's growth. Trust liberates us from the endless treadmill of the mind, giving us hope that there is a better, brighter way to view and rise above challenges. It is the proverbial light at the end of the tunnel of darkness in which we feel trapped. My advice is to trust that the higher mind of Spirit is *always* working in your favor, even if you cannot see that in the moment. Your soul is consistently speaking to you and continually evolving.

The fear of trust is frequently based on previous violations of that trust by others or through circumstances in life. Trust requires vulnerability, which is difficult to embrace when we've been hurt in the past, suffered loss, endured abuse, or are scarred by trauma. In response, people naturally shield themselves for self-protection. This keeps one safe, but is terribly lonely, limiting, depressing, and ultimately self-defeating. These emotions are wakeup calls that we are unbalanced, out of touch with the vitality of life, and stuck in the past. To heal, a new perspective is in order — and yes, it requires trust.

A common misperception is equating vulnerability to weakness. It is *not* weakness, at least spiritually speaking. To the contrary, being vulnerable means that we are wise, willing, and secure enough to align with a force much greater than our personal self — a power that works in us, through us, and for us. Consider this: Since all souls share the common intent to reunite with the Creator, all life experiences, without exception, lead to that end and only that end. Whether we choose to add 1000 extra miles to that ultimate destination by making self-defeating choices or quicken the pace by aligning ourselves with higher consciousness, the destination is the same. Trusting that Spirit loves us unconditionally accelerates the journey and brings peace.

Open Your Heart to Trust

Think of a time your trust in someone or something was violated. Viewing this with hindsight, what did the circumstance reveal to you about yourself? Did you have unrealistic expectations? Did you ignore your gut perceptions? What did you learn from the experience?

If you find it difficult to trust, start by connecting to the anchor of Spirit within. This is very easy to do, one day at a time. Sit quietly several times a day and focus on your breath as it enters and exits your body. Next, move your awareness to your heart. Imagine the breath enters your heart, and gently opens and expands it, pulling you deeper and deeper.

Thoughts will naturally arise during this time. Do not try to dismiss them; simply notice them and refocus on your breath as it circulates in your heart. If you wish, you may also visualize a rose in the heart with its petals tightly closed at the start of the exercise.

As you continue breathing trust into this area, witness the rose slowly opening, petal by petal to reveal its stunning beauty. Keep this image alive in your mind's eye throughout the day.

When you feel a small amount of trust arising, test the waters where large investments of trust are not required. Share your feelings with a good friend, ask for a small favor from someone or give a modest donation to an organization. These may not seem like much, but they help to (re)build trust. Each time you allow yourself to be open, you strengthen a base of trust that helps to erase doubt, anxiety and fear.

Surmounting Fear and Anxiety

Most of us are well acquainted with fear because it is a universal human emotion that takes various forms and intensity, depending on our personal makeup and the situation that triggers it. But here's something of value to ask when it arises: How can we make fear into our ally instead of our enemy? How can something paralyzing be used positively for spiritual growth? What is fear's message to us?

Fear is born when we step (voluntarily or not) outside of our comfort zone. Its evolutionary purpose is to keep us safe from some type of danger. When we are in its grip, we feel anxious, unsafe, uncertain, and unstable. From the beginning of time, humans have encountered fear when confronting animals in the wild, through the threat of violence, injury or death, in wars, while enduring natural disasters, and in the displacement or destruction of our homes. All of these circumstances share two elements: a change in one's former, familiar condition, and the subsequent efforts to cope with the unknown that result from that change.

Although change comes relatively easily for some, most people fear change because it upsets one's sense of familiarity, safety, and controllable conditions in life. It usually feels more secure to remain in the known rather than confront the unknown. Will we be able to cope with the new circumstances? The truth is that most change becomes less threatening once we adapt to it. Once again, these circumstances call upon us to trust that the new situation will present us with opportunities to grow, coupled with a healthy dose of time for necessary adjustment. Note that this doesn't mean that we necessarily *like* new, different circumstances. Trusting that we have the ability to adapt to them, however, helps to dissipate fear.

In mediumship readings, my spirit team has revealed that certain souls require intense acclimation to adjust to the spirit world after death. Sometimes this is due to the person's fear of death; others had no belief that there is indeed an afterlife. In the case of fear, souls are soothed by spirit healers who encourage them to rest while they adjust to the new conditions of the spirit world. As acclimation continues, fear dissipates.

In my numerous case files, some souls have communicated that once in spirit, they discover there is nothing to fear. They regret the wasted time and energy fretting about death when they were in physical life. I believe these types of messages are seminal in helping others when death approaches, and this is precisely why they are brought forth during readings. These souls want loved ones to know that there is nothing to fear about death, and that the spirit world is as much a home as earth. In fact, it is our real home.

The origin of fear is the rational mind. There it is amplified and distorted by repetitive thoughts that build in intensity. The mind often finds something to be fearful about. However, it can be transcended by focusing on the consciousness of the soul, that "space" between mind-generated, fearful thoughts. It is impossible to find deep peace through the mind because that is not where it resides. It is realized by connecting with the soul's consciousness, the inner sanctuary. At the end of this section is an exercise you can do to visit this space whenever you wish.

As I write this, anxiety (an offshoot of fear) is pervasive among populations worldwide. Young people, especially, report experiencing more anxiety than ever before.[1] Although it's always existed, in the last several years the number of people suffering with anxiety has greatly accelerated due to the 2020 pandemic and the resulting upheavals. People felt unsafe due to sudden, unexpected, fundamental changes and interruptions to their everyday lives. Many experienced anxiety about contracting the virus. Connecting with family and friends, visiting those who were vulnerable to or sick with the virus, attending entertainment venues, going to the gym, and routine grocery shopping were strongly discouraged by government and healthcare professionals, or eliminated entirely. Many older people experienced isolation and loneliness during this time. Although these conditions have largely subsided, the anxiety they created has not. In fact, it continues to rise. During the last several years, I have personally connected with more anxiety-ridden people than ever before in my practice, even though the global pandemic has wound down.

During these sessions, my spirit team recommends spiritual practices such as mindfulness and body awareness to help individuals cope. Anxiety arises when we feel a lack of control, apprehension, and uncertainty over situations. Restlessness, desperation, hopelessness, and depression often accompany states of anxiety. How can we mitigate these uncomfortable states? One answer is to have the awareness that we *do* have control of our reactions by connecting to the anchor of Spirit to help alleviate them. The remedy is not "out there" but within each of us.

Because I am naturally sensitive to energy, I've been keenly aware of a generalized, underlying, persistent anxiety in the collective human consciousness that arose during the pandemic and is rampant today. In addition to concerns about the illness itself, I've sensed people's uneasiness about trusting government health agencies, political leadership, monetary inflation, homelessness, crime, drug addiction, the refugee crisis, and escalating violence.

Anxiety is a natural reaction to these troubling conditions because few of them are under our direct control. One solution to reducing anxiety about these crises is to do what is possible as individuals in small, manageable ways. Every action taken by one person adds to the whole of ameliorating them. In this way, one person does indeed make a difference. Instead of viewing seemingly insurmountable issues as hopeless and allowing yourself to be overwhelmed by them, do what you are capable of. For example, if you are concerned about the increase in homelessness, volunteer or donate to help those in need. If you are worried about crime, attend local town hall meetings to address this issue. Does anxiety about societal division cause you distress? Do what you can to promote understanding and unity in your local community. If we all sit back and do nothing, problems intensify. Transformation begins with the individual and spreads outward. Power for resolution builds thereafter when individuals come together to effect change. There is no other way.

Unfortunately, some people turn to dangerous drugs to alleviate fear and anxiety. Alarmingly, addiction to opioids is likewise an epidemic in current times. The devastation that addiction causes is evident in every city and town in America (as well as other nations). In the last several years, I have connected with innumerable people who have lost loved ones to fentanyl and heroin overdoses. Several of these involved communications with souls who died instantly the first time they used the drugs.

In these instances, I cannot adequately express how overwhelmingly heartbreaking it is to speak with their families and friends who suffer immeasurable grief. I've often wished that everyone who considers turning to drugs and government administrations who do little to stop the infiltration of drugs into the country could witness the absolute horror that addiction creates by listening to the stories of families who are grieving loved ones who died from them. One of the few consolations for these families is sharing their stories to help others who face the same circumstances.

What is at the root of anxiety? Simply put, worry and fear about the future, whether tomorrow, next week, or next year. Yet all we have available is right here, right now. Changing our focus from past and future to the present moment reduces anxiety. Practicing this shift in awareness aids in rewiring our brain from hypervigilance to relaxed observation of the anxious thoughts. This is not to say being anxious is wrong all the time; it's a natural, protective reaction from our instincts. Yet when it becomes crippling, it reduces the ability to function and diminishes the quality of life. The good news is it can be diminished by feeling it, accepting it, and then transcending it.

I've personally experienced several severe bouts of anxiety triggered by certain circumstances beyond my control. These were compelling wakeup calls that led me to examine my reactivity to external events and the perceived need to be in control of all circumstances in my life. During one of these struggles, I had what could be called a nervous breakdown. My thoughts spiraled out of control, making the proverbial mountain out of a molehill. Soon I became paralyzed by these fearful thoughts, leaving me unable to do my work. This, I learned, is called *catastrophizing*, where the worst possible outcome of a situation is played over and over in the mind, causing ever-increasing, debilitating anxiety. I felt overpowered by these thoughts and became physically ill. If you ever doubt the intense power of your thoughts, try stopping the "voice" of your thoughts when they gain momentum. You will quickly discover just how relentless and potent they are. Yet there is a way to break free.

Using the tools of mindfulness and body awareness, coupled with mild medication and psychotherapy released me from this destructive mind monologue. I will forever be grateful for the healing I obtained during this stressful time, most notably through daily breathing practices. I've recommended these to multiple clients since then. A bonus of using this type of meditation is its easy adaptability to any stressful situation. Your breath is always available in any given moment.

Fear cannot stop you if you recognize it for what it is: an invitation to go deeper, to explore, examine, and investigate what patterns of habitual thought you're holding. It's a signal that you are about to enter previously unexplored territory within your own psyche. Most fear does not arise from the real threat of imminent danger but from *believing* there is or will be such danger. The old adage, "Feel the fear and do it anyway," is sound advice. Fear cannot obliterate your inner landscape of peace, which is always there at your core. Reframe it as an engagement with your spiritual growth. In this way, fear becomes an ally, not an enemy.

Being Still Is Essential

The necessity of stillness cannot be overstated when coping not only with fear and anxiety, but for achieving peace of mind — a rare commodity in today's chaotic world. In our fast-paced modern lifestyle, it's vital to our mental, emotional, and physical well-being to take time every day to withdraw from the external world into stillness.

Until I began my journey of spiritual awareness, I couldn't understand why I felt flustered, stressed, drained, and exhausted after being in crowds, noisy public places, or after talking to certain people. Somewhere along the way, I realized that regular quietness is essential for me to be at my best. This need to retreat into oneself to be comfortable is called *introversion* in psychology. Whatever you may call it, many people function optimally while spending time removed from the hustle and bustle of the outside world.

But *everyone* benefits from being still, although many people refuse to make time to do it. Some are so addicted to drama, upsets, and catastrophes in life that even the suggestion of being still is highly uncomfortable to them. I sense that this is due to fear of examining oneself and being alone with one's thoughts. What may be discovered in the silence is potentially more threatening than being perpetually busy, constantly moving about and in chaos. People may feel as if something is fundamentally wrong with them or that they are missing out on life if they take time out to be still. Continually engaging with the outside world and others leaves little time for honest introspection. If we don't take that necessary time, illness, accidents, anxiety, fatigue, and mental breakdowns may *force* us to take it.

Exploring Beyond Your Thoughts

Below are easy methods to savor stillness, create time alone, replenish vitality, relish being alone, and gain clarity from your soul.

(There are several other methods you can use to practice mindfulness. I list these in Chapter Nine for your use.)

Breathwork

The easiest way to do this is to close your eyes and simply place your attention on your breath. Doing this basic exercise several times a day "resets" your consciousness and reduces stress. In my breathing practice, I feel as if I'm visiting another world when I go inside, one that is gentle, welcoming, and nourishing. Returning to "normal" consciousness then feels transformed, more relaxed. This is why I call mindfulness a reset.

Body Awareness

Body awareness is when you shift your attention from one body part to another, starting with the feet and moving up the trunk to the head. Breathe into each body part, holding the intent for peace, relaxation, and healing with each breath. Then hold your entire body in your focus and feel the life stream flowing through it.

Focus

Choose an external object (anything nearby will suffice), center your gaze on it, and study all the details of what you observe — the color, texture, design, and size. Become lost in the object. Imagine what it would feel like if you picked up the object. See the object apart from the past meaning you've given to it. Observe it through fresh perspective.

You can also use this method with a small piece of food, such as a raisin, nut, or piece of chocolate. Place it into your mouth, and feel its texture and flavor. When you chew it, place your attention on the sensations that arise. We rarely enjoy food because we are in a hurry to eat, at times so quickly that our brain doesn't register when we are satiated. Mindful eating slows down the process for you to savor the food and enjoy the moment. (Also refer to the second exercise at the end of this chapter, Practice Being in Present Time.)

Engage with Infants, Children, Animals, and Nature

Have you ever considered why many of us are enchanted by babies and animals? In addition to being adorable, they emanate purity, innocence, and playfulness — qualities that resonate with our innermost being. They speak the language of the soul. Babies and animals radiate the presence of Spirit without judgment, thinking, analyzing, or awareness of time.

We possess these very same qualities in our own souls, although they are frequently buried beneath our thoughts. If you do not have the opportunity to engage live and in person with children, gaze at photos or videos and allow them to touch, captivate and enliven this deepest part of your consciousness. By doing so, you are resonating with the purity of your soul.

Animals attract us because they display alert consciousness, the state of being we likewise possess but often ignore due to thought and analysis. Observe a bird listening intently, a chipmunk pausing to glean information about its surroundings, or a rabbit's fixed posture to elude predators, and you will see how animals exist in present-time awareness. They are not thinking of last week or tomorrow; they are fully present in the moment.

Nature also reminds us of the stillness within. Birds chirping, the soothing sensation of a gentle breeze rustling our hair, the sight of colorful flowers and trees, the smell of springtime, the calming gurgle of a stream, or the hum of crickets reflect the boundless life force that flows through all of creation. You and I are part of that very same life stream. Nature exists without analysis, planning, or artificial time constructs. It is perfect in its expression, except for where humans have interfered with its natural order.

Appreciation of a tree, flower, or plant elevates our consciousness to its natural state and also positively affects the life forms that we appreciate. How is this possible? Studies of the effects of human consciousness on water by Dr. Masaru Emoto and others give us a clue into this phenomenon.[2] Through his extensive research and large-scale experiments worldwide, Emoto demonstrated that water molecules form varying crystalline patterns in response to thoughts, words, and music that are "injected" into them. These experiments showed that water has the ability to replicate information and emotion from its surroundings.

Using natural water (from a spring, not filtered from a tap), Emoto exposed it to various types of vibration (thought, words, and sound), froze the water samples, then studied them under magnification. What Emoto found, for example, is that thoughts of hate directed at test samples of water caused the molecules to be misshapen, jagged, and irregular in appearance. In contrast, words and thoughts of love, benevolence, and good will, along with soothing, uplifting music, produced intricate patterns of exquisite beauty, symmetrical in appearance and well formed. Although some scientists have disputed these findings, I believe that they hold validity when applying the study's results to our physical bodies, which consist of 99% water. Overall, Emoto's studies offer convincing evidence of both humans' influence on the environment and, conversely, its effects on us.

Take Time to Be Alone

As mentioned previously, withdrawing from others on a regular basis is something everyone needs to do in order to maintain a state of well-being. Finding a balance between engaging with others and with the external world will change your quality of life for the better. Even small changes such as dedicating an area of a room for spiritual practices such as mindfulness and meditation enables you to go on retreat from the busyness of life.

Go for a walk by yourself and bask in the silence. Garden. Write in a journal. Draw or paint. These solitary activities are forms of meditation because they allow perceptions to arise outside of the thinking mind. Build alone time into your daily life and see how much difference it makes to your mental and emotional health.

Growing up, I spent countless hours by myself in the sanctuary of my bedroom listening to music and reading. There I could explore my innermost self through thinking and imagining without interruption. In those days, I wasn't familiar with the term "introvert" much less the constructs of rational thought. I simply recognized how comfortable and enjoyable it was to spend hours alone.

One day when I was running late for a job, my dad, who had grown frustrated with my escapism, said, "Carole, you'd better come out of your dream world and get used to the real world!" His words stung me. I felt as if I'd been slapped since I saw nothing wrong with what I was doing. It was natural for me to spend time by myself. Decades later, I've come to accept that it's essential to my well-being to spend time alone.

Stop Glorifying Busyness

In addition to the epidemics of fear, anxiety and drug addiction that are plaguing our society, it seems that we have a modern obsession with being perpetually busy. Today, people claim to be too busy to respond to invitations, return emails and phone calls, engage in conversations, visit family and friends, or enjoy time away from work. Being continually busy leaves little time for relaxation, much less introspection. Being busy has become an excuse to be detached, ungracious, uncaring, unresponsive, and downright lazy! Do not prioritize busyness over meaningful connection with others. As evidenced in multiple readings, those in spirit express regret over not spending time with family and friends due to working long hours and occupying themselves with other tasks. Life can be overwhelming at times and we all need periodic breaks to refresh, renew, and relax.

Don't Fall Prey to Hopelessness

One of the easiest things to fall prey to when we feel lost, confused, grief-stricken, undermined, or uncertain is hopelessness. Our minds may repeatedly tell us this is the way "it" is and will be forever. Given that one of the mind's attributes is to immediately race to the worst possible outcome of any circumstance, it's easy to understand how losing hope can spiral out of control. However, if we pull back from this false mindset and recognize this deflating outlook for what it is — a fantasy — we open the door to hope, even if it is a brief flicker. That flicker catches fire the longer we embrace it; despair lessens. Just as negative thoughts build in intensity, so can positive ones. Making a commitment to allow hope to flow from your soul is vital in personal and spiritual transformation.

To be perfectly direct, adopting hopelessness in response to life circumstances is often an excuse to do nothing about them. Additionally, it's a strong form of resistance to the reality of personal responsibility in taking ownership of one's thoughts, actions, and behaviors. After all, if we decide to label a situation as hopeless, there's not much (if anything) that we can do to change it. Consider that this is a cop-out which denies the existence of free will and the power to change our thoughts about the situation. The mind dialogue of hopelessness goes something like this:

- *I'll never land a job as rewarding as the one I lost. I'm working at a job I hate going to every day, just to survive. I've applied to dozens of places, but nothing comes through for me. Ever.*
- Or, *I've had several bad love relationships. I'm a loser in love. I must have been born to be alone. I thought I'd be with someone by now! What the hell is wrong with me anyway? When will I be happy?*

How do you feel after reading these lines? Hopeful? Probably not! I've done multiple life-guidance sessions with people who had this self-defeating attitude. They wanted me to tune in to see what the future held in terms of job and relationship success yet they walked around consistently with a highly charged negative narrative about themselves. Curiously, it never entered their minds to aspire to the much higher consciousness of hope.

At times, clients become upset and frustrated when no magical answers to these types of questions are forthcoming in sessions. They expect all problems to be cured in the course of an hour, without any effort on their behalf. No one will miraculously come down from the sky and grant us happiness, love, money, or a career. The future (which doesn't exist yet) is determined by choices made *today*.

No honest, legitimate, genuine medium or psychic can predict events with 100% accuracy because that would subvert the reality of clients' free will. I make this fact crystal clear before and during readings. On top of this, I cannot (nor can anyone) bear responsibility for people's lives and the choices they make. That's a sure way to become arrogant, controlling, and "needed" — all of which are unethical in mediumship and psychic services. You alone own your life, your mind, and your choices. You direct your life.

Hope is created and bolstered by forming an intent of plausible actions and outcomes in a given situation. It's a good idea to write these down to firmly plant them in your consciousness. For example, what do you want to have happen in your life? How do you choose to feel? Place these written reminders where you will see them every day. Then, focus on them with unwavering trust that Spirit is *always* working on your behalf, even if it does not appear so. What we give energy to through our thoughts expands, because thought *is* energy. We cannot control others and outside events. We *can* control our perception of and reaction to them.

Reconsider Your Concept of Time

Related to hope is the struggle that people often have with the concept of time. Of all the questions that come up during readings, "when" (will this or that happen) is by far the most common. Further, the passage of time doesn't automatically guarantee that we'll be energetically and emotionally prepared for whatever is desired. People create artificial timelines for something to occur, and when it doesn't, hopelessness ensues.

What they do not realize is that falling into hopelessness negates the manifestation of desires. If we believe something will not occur, we do not create the conditions and space for it to occur. To experience anything, our consciousness must match that of what we wish to experience. This is the most difficult aspect of transformation for most to grasp. I believe part of this is also due to resistance (conscious or not) to change.

Four Qualities for Personal Transformation

How, then, is change accomplished? As mentioned earlier, four qualities are necessary for personal transformation: Gut honesty, surrender, trust, and patience.

Honesty requires the courage to fearlessly go within, remove the filter of our own ego, and take a personal inventory of our strengths and weaknesses. This gives clarity and the ability to observe oneself without pretense. For example, have you ever desired change and then regretted it when it occurred? Perhaps you realized that it was not what you wanted or needed after all. Deep soul-searching helps you to appraise your true desires and needs while contemplating change. During this phase, you may also imagine in vivid detail what your desired experience will be like.

Surrender is necessary to accept your life exactly as it is in the here and now. This eliminates resistance to change and smooths the pathway to create your vision on a fresh, new canvas. It entails stepping into a space of acceptance of what your current experience is now.

Trust gives hope, stability, and endurance throughout the process. It means admitting we possess unfettered access to an intelligence beyond our limited mind.

Patience during the process is vital to keep the vision alive. Living one day at a time is the best approach to take. (We'll explore self-appraisal further in Part Two.)

Create a Vision Board

Make your personal vision board by pasting cut-out images from magazines or other printed materials on a large poster board. Place it in a location that you will see it every day.

Fuel your images with emotions like joy, peacefulness, relaxation, fulfillment, zest. Trust that these visions will indeed manifest for you.

During another one of my trips to the spiritualist community of Lilydale, New York, I took a workshop on creating a personal vision of desired experiences, as outlined in the exercise, above. At that time, visions boards were popular — large poster boards covered with photos cut from magazines which mirror the creator's desired circumstances. In my case, I pasted photos of a lovely ranch house with stunning interior woodwork, a loving couple in an embrace, a diamond engagement ring, a dog, and a pair of smiling lips (to symbolize happiness) on my poster board, among other images. We were instructed to place these in a location at home where they would be visible to us every day.

As time passed, I made looking at my vision board part of my daily routine. During the next several years, one by one, I received most of what was pictured on the board. I got engaged, married, bought a lovely ranch house, and am happy/ smiling most days. Some people might say I was lucky, but I do not believe luck exists. We receive what we believe. We create through the thoughts we employ. Believe you are worthy of *all* good experiences in life and you will soon see your life transform. You are well on your way!

Practice Being in Present Time

Choose an ordinary, routine activity and "be in" that activity while doing it. Examples are bathing, washing your hands, brushing your teeth, doing the dishes, or running the vacuum.

Place all of your attention on the activity. What do you notice? What sensations arise? How does this focus differ from how you normally engage with the activity?

Part Two

Surrender: Releasing Resistance to Your Soul's Intention

On a balmy afternoon in September 1984, I kneel by a dresser in a small, stark motel room that I'm renting. It's been 10 months since I stopped drinking but my life is still unsettled, tangled, and littered with remnants of prior chaos. I attend several 12-step meetings per week yet I remain uncertain, angry, and discouraged. I have no job, despite applying for various openings. I've got few friends beyond the ones I see at the meetings. *They probably won't stick around*, I pessimistically think. *I thought things were supposed to get better when I became sober, not worse!*

Deeply frustrated and disillusioned, I decide to halfheartedly get on my knees and ask my Higher Power for help on the rigorous journey of recovery from alcoholism. During the past year, I'd listened countless times to others in 12-step meetings describe this act of surrender and humility, but I'd never done it myself. I remember these individuals saying that the posture of being on one's knees made them aware that there's something far more powerful than themselves, a presence that is always listening and willing to help.

I'm too strong, too proud and too smart, I believed. Until now. I'm flat out of hope. It's time. *Maybe, just maybe*, I think, *this surrender stuff works. I doubt it, but I'll give it a shot.*

Alone in the room, I'm startlingly self-conscious. I feel simultaneously awkward and nervous, relieved that no one can see me doing this. I bend down and begin to ramble to Spirit: *I don't know where I'm headed with my life but I desperately need help to find my way. I feel alone, confused, and scared. I need a job. Please bring a job my way. It's what I need to feel good and worthy again. I need friends, too. I promise to go to 12-step meetings, but I need to work and have support!*

I repeat my pleas just in case the "something" doesn't hear me. And then I cry so hard and deep that it feels as if my gut and heart are going to explode. I admit that I can't manage my life on my own. I surrender.

I wish I could tell you that my life immediately improved, but I'd be dishonest. I'd like to say that I had an epiphany that day, but I didn't. It would have been lovely if angels appeared in that dingy motel room to assure me that everything would work out, but there were none. I simply let go of the need to live life in the same way that had led to the misery I desperately sought to release. It was amazingly simple.

What I didn't know on that day is that I opened a door to unimaginable *power* when I surrendered. Not the false power of my demanding, manipulative, self-centered, singular ego; rather, genuine power that emanates from the higher, all-knowing Source residing within the sanctuary of my soul. That day was the beginning of my *spiritual* recovery, of relinquishing the iron grip of false control that my ego held onto tenaciously for years. Thus began the process of liberation from my ingrained, self-imposed comfort zones into a new way of being.

Many people believe that surrendering indicates defeat, weakness, and vulnerability. In some situations, this is true, such as when we give in to something (or someone) that is not in our best interest. But when we break through our own resistance into living life from a higher perspective in collaboration with Spirit, we attain authentic power that moves mountains. Paradoxically, surrender is the best choice to make when we feel helpless because it releases resistance to our soul's intentions. Acceptance of everything just as it is allows us to ponder our next steps on the journey through the guidance of our soul's higher consciousness.

In this book part, you'll learn about how life challenges beckon us to explore the bridge of transformation, along with the stages of metamorphosis and the pitfalls to avoid along the way. As you read the stories of people who courageously met life on its own terms during dark nights, set foot on the bridge of transformation, and moved forward, consider your own life challenges and what lessons they've delivered. If you are currently immersed in a dark night, take comfort in knowing you'll make it through — wiser, stronger, and more resilient.

In Chapter 6, you'll read about the immutable, spiritual laws that ensure a balanced, harmonious, and righteous life if we align ourselves with them. I've included a discussion of these eternal principles because it's critical to know that there is a living, sublime intelligence that supersedes our own ego, personality, self-centeredness and, importantly, human-made laws. This life force flows through all of creation without human-imposed, artificially constructed boundaries. We cannot exist apart from it because we *are* it.

There is no such thing as "my truth" or "your truth" as used in popular vernacular. There is only *The Higher Truth* which does not discriminate, divide, categorize, or show deference to one individual over another. Nor does it differentiate between species. It has nothing to do with gender. Each of us is equally valuable and irreplaceable in the eyes of this greater intelligence. Each is worthy, cherished and unconditionally loved. We are not segregated by particular groups, races, religions, or cultures. We are inextricably united in *one* consciousness, regardless of external differences. When we surrender to this truth, we allow the wisdom of the soul to lead the way.

4

The Bridge: Stages of Spiritual Transformation

One can choose to go back toward safety or forward toward growth. Growth must be chosen again and again; fear must be overcome again and again.
~ Abraham Maslow

The phone rings in my office, signaling my 1:30 p.m. appointment. On the other end of the call is Sara, who had previously told me that she is seeking life guidance in our scheduled session. After exchanging pleasantries, I say my prayer and tune into her life energy. I'm immediately aware of emotional trauma trapped in her energy field.

"There are past experiences you're carrying that feel very painful," I begin. "These appear to go back to your childhood. I sense you are still carrying these old wounds. I'm aware of abuse. Does this make sense?" I ask.

"Yes," she responds in a hushed voice. (I can barely hear her and ask her to speak up. Clear voice enunciation is vital in readings since the vibration of voice emanates an abundance of intuitive information to me.) As we continue, I sense even further that Sara's current emotional upset is deeply rooted in a distressing childhood.

"Yeah, growing up was horrible," she admits. "My mom drank heavily and my dad cheated on my mom. But that's not what I need guidance on today," she says, quickly steering me away from that topic. "I'd like to know why everyone I've cared about leaves me. I've been married twice before my current marriage and both men divorced me to be with someone else.

I was blindsided with no warning. They were cheating on me. Now I feel as if it's happening again with my current husband. I don't trust him when he's out. I'm really scared he's going to leave, too. Can you tell me what to do? I'm exhausted and can't go through this again!"

Listening to my intuition and the guidance of my spirit team, I know that Sara's current predicament of unhealthy relationships stems from the anguish she endured growing up. Despite her resistance, I press on, trusting my higher guidance.

"What you've gone through in your marriages and what you are currently going through are the result of unresolved emotions from your past. I know you don't want to talk about it or face it but that's the only way you'll be able to move beyond this harmful pattern. It's time to get in touch with those old wounds and rewrite your life story."

After a moment of silence, Sara sighs, "Okay, okay. But I've already dealt with that! My parents are both dead and I forgave them a long time ago. What does this have to do with now?"

I feel her impatience. "A lot. In fact, everything ... if you want to change your life and unhappiness. There is still residue of that old pattern of unworthiness, the message you absorbed in your childhood. Subconsciously, you believe you are unlovable. Also, you were not emotionally supported by your parents. You're repeating those patterns by attracting relationships with men who do not value you and who leave you."

Next, I become aware of Sara's mother and father connecting with me from the spirit world, impressing me with their behavior during physical life. "Your mother says that she was an alcoholic. She demeaned you, screamed at you and ignored you, she says. Your dad went along with the program by not confronting her about her abusiveness. He didn't step up and protect you from her either. Your mom's come to you long before this reading today to communicate her deep regret for all of this since she's seen how this has affected you."

"Yeah, she did all those things. It was horrible. I ran away from home a couple of times to escape her abuse. I love my dad, but I could never figure out why he supported her! I felt if he loved me, he would have protected me. In a way, I'm relieved to know she sees how much she hurt me. But what does this have to do with my marriage today?" she asks again.

"Think about it," I reply. "How could you possibly have a healthy adult relationship when you continue to play the old tapes from long ago? These are the patterns you've absorbed. That's some heavy baggage. I know you've forgiven your parents, but you've internalized their treatment of you and made it your own. They more or less abandoned you emotionally. Clear, delete, and cancel all of those outworn self-identifications. They are false beliefs. This will make a huge difference. You will also benefit from psychotherapy, even if it's for a short time," I advise.

At the end of the session, Sara agrees to seek counseling. Several months later, she emailed me to say that she was doing much better, although she had ended her marriage. She felt it was the best thing to do due to the lack of trust. Sara was still discovering a new way of life, but was relieved to finally confront the unhealthy patterns that she had absorbed from years ago. She was undergoing transformation and awakening spiritually. For the first time in her life, Sara discovered that she no longer had to be a prisoner of her harrowing past.

I chose Sara's story to begin this chapter about the stages of spiritual transformation because it is representative of multiple life guidance sessions I've given where outworn mental and emotional patterns — many originating in childhood — continue to sabotage individuals years later until the patterns are addressed and transformed. These clients come to sessions to discover how they can feel better. Many do not know what is causing them distress or what needs to change; they simply know they are profoundly unhappy with their current lives.

At times, these deeply rooted patterns are not only from childhood, but also from past incarnations, which have been carried by the soul into the present life where they can be confronted and resolved. This requires my peering into the soul's akashic files (the totality of the soul's experiences) to determine the origin of the patterns. I've written extensively about these files and their relevance to self-discovery and healing in my book, *Wisdom from the Spirit World*. Once the origins of patterns are discovered, the restraints are loosened, a new perception emerges, and healing occurs.

As we move through life, we experience various transitions during which we shed an old way of being for a new one. Birth (transition from the spirit world), adolescence, graduation, higher education, employment, partnership, marriage, the birth of children, retirement, old age and, ultimately, death (return to the spirit world) are the significant changes that the majority of people experience throughout life. Although each of these is unique as far as the age and manner in which we undergo these shifts, as well as the mindset we bring to them and how we adapt to them, they share a common factor: the movement from one state of being to another. The old must be released to accept the new.

This chapter focuses specifically on the phenomenon of *spiritual* transformation, the transition to a higher state of consciousness from a lower one. This type of transformation is either initiated organically by the soul in its ever-evolving journey towards reunion with the Creator or through wakeup calls (as previously discussed).

In any transition we go through in life, spiritual transformation is possible, although it does not necessarily occur in all cases. Spiritual transformation is frequently initiated and accompanied by some form of loss and/or trauma, such as addiction, abuse, betrayal, death of a loved one, loss of happiness, or loss of physical or mental health. To alleviate these or to evolve from them, change is required. In addition, customary life transitions (listed above) are much easier to navigate when we embrace and rely on a higher level of spiritual consciousness. It is a secure foundation that can be depended upon during various life transitions.

Let me be clear: These are not superficial changes such as losing weight, buying new clothes, changing hairstyles, purchasing a new house, or making more money; they are critical changes that transform the deepest core of the self. Typically, they involve the release of thought and behavior patterns that have grown stale, limiting, self-defeating, unproductive and, in some cases, life threatening.

Intuition comes into play preceding and during such transitions when we receive direction from our soul that is intended to move us to higher ground, so to speak. These often appear through feelings, subtle or intense, that something within needs to be given careful attention. I list many of these under the first stage of transformation, below. The need for change can also appear through fatigue, illness, depression, or anxiety. All of these indicate that we are at odds with the natural, harmonious state of the soul. They beckon us to higher ground.

If you've ever found yourself reacting to various situations in life with the same caliber of thoughts, emotions, and actions, chances are you're locked into habitual patterns. Many times, we are not conscious of our reactions because we're so accustomed to them that they've become second nature. Thoughts such as *That's just the way I am, It's justified for me to feel this way, I can never win in life* or *I am unlovable* are examples of beliefs that indicate we are not living in accordance with the true nature of the soul. This habit of self-deflating thinking has to be examined and changed during spiritual transformation in order to reach a higher state of consciousness.

Stages of Spiritual Transformation

There are three distinct stages of spiritual consciousness transformation. To help you better understand these, I use the analogy of crossing a bridge as representative of the process. I was first introduced to this metaphor years ago in a book about Arthur Ford, a well-known medium and Spiritualist during the early part of the 20th century, *Extension of Life: Arthur Ford Speaks*, written by one of my teachers at Delphi University, Patricia Hayes. The author (who claims to have obtained the book's teachings from Ford in spirit) applies the bridge analogy to both life transitions and death.[1] I've adapted the concept here, using my own words, personal understanding, observations, and experience from thousands of sessions.

Stage One: Contemplation

Imagine that you are standing on one end of a bridge. This image can be any way you envision it; use your power of imagination so that the condition of the bridge you imagine matches the change and pathway you're about to navigate.

Look at the bridge. Is it wobbly, bumpy, steep, old and broken, or smooth, flat, shiny and new? You have not yet stepped onto it; you are merely looking at its condition from your current vantage point (your present consciousness).

From this perspective, begin to contemplate your current position, how you feel about its condition (is the "ground" hard, uncomfortable, unstable, steep, or rocky?) and how well it is serving you in the progression of your life. Does it need to be replaced or simply upgraded?

Of all the stages, this is the one that requires the most unfiltered, raw honesty. It's helpful to write your insights in a journal to give clarity. Your contemplation questions may be the ones listed below. (Note: I use the word "situation" to describe any and all circumstances regarding your current state of being.)

- How well does my current situation serve my life values?
- What have I outgrown in this situation?

- If I stay here (without making any changes), how am I likely to feel?
- What are probable ways I can change? What resources and tools can I use?
- Who can I turn to for support during this change?
- Who has already successfully crossed the bridge and can serve as a role model for me?
- What is a realistic vision of my new way of being? How would my life look and feel after traversing the bridge?

After asking the last question, begin to contemplate what it would be like to cross the bridge. Looking across it, ponder the condition, width, and length of the bridge and what will be required on your behalf to cross it. Note any feelings that come up when you consider crossing the bridge, such as fear, uncertainty, relief, or happiness.

Feelings that commonly arise during this contemplative stage are restlessness, lack of fulfillment, boredom, anxiety, mild depression, confusion, regret, uncertainty, discouragement, and fear. You may experience all of these or several of them. Instead of viewing them as "bad," consider them as natural indicators of your impending change for the better. Know that these feelings usually lessen once the stage of movement begins.

What inner qualities do you need to call upon to make the move? Once this process of contemplation is complete and you've examined the bridge from all perspectives, you are ready to progress into the second stage.

Stage Two: Reflection

You are now at the pivotal point of stepping onto the bridge. But before you do, consider what you wish to bring along during this change and what you desire to leave behind. Evaluate your life up until now. Reflect on the past to determine your intent for the new space on the other side of the bridge. You may ask:

- What are my achievements, skills, strengths, and triumphs?
- What beliefs, attitudes, and emotions brought desired results?
- What choices have brought undesired or painful circumstances?
- Which core thoughts and beliefs have brought me unhappiness?
- Which core thoughts have contributed to my well-being?

To use the example of recovery from addiction to alcohol or drugs, consider what thoughts, emotions, and behaviors need to be examined and changed to live successfully without substances. What external and internal triggers (stress, people, relationships, places) to addiction need to be abandoned? When you first used substances, what were your thoughts and feelings? What positive qualities do you possess that will be beneficial to your new space on the other side of the bridge?

For instance, you may be a determined person, one who does not give up easily. This would be a quality to take with you on the journey because it will assist you in staying with the recovery process. Perhaps you're a friendly, outgoing person, which will help you in bonding with a support or 12-step group, meeting a sponsor, or sharing your personal experiences with others during recovery. Again, it's helpful to inventory these in a journal for clarity and future reference.

Make a list of major events in your past that come up during introspection. What was your reaction to these? What response did you give? Which emotions were present? What did you learn about yourself from these events? Finally, how can you improve your perspective upon the past?

The reflection stage also involves the formation of your intent for the new consciousness you've chosen to adopt. Intent must be clarified in order to avoid duplication of the past. If you do not form an intent, you will likely attract circumstances identical to the past ones.

An intent is a plan, a blueprint, a strategy for your new way of being. Focusing on this unwaveringly allows it to be firmly planted in your consciousness. I suggest writing your intent on a sheet of paper in large letters and placing it where you will see it *every day*; on a bathroom mirror, for example. Use positive, affirmative words in writing it: "I am staying sober one day at a time."

Because thoughts are the cause of all we create and experience in life, it's vital to examine them in depth. If we desire to see new results, we must create corresponding thoughts and intents that match those desires, or they will not appear in reality. The reflective stage involves differentiating thoughts that support your desired results from those which do not. This involves your power of choice and free will. You create your new consciousness. You captain the way across the bridge.

Once you've determined what you're taking with you across the bridge, it's time to step onto it. This is when you will probably feel intense, diverse emotions; fear, relief, confusion, joy, doubt, enthusiasm, anger, and a desire to be reclusive are all possible when the first step is taken. It's noteworthy to remember that emotions are fleeting; spiritual transformation is not. Do not allow temporary emotions to eclipse your resolve to move ahead. Allow and acknowledge all feelings as they arise but keep moving.

Continuing with the example of addiction recovery, your first step onto the bridge may be attending a 12-step group, booking a stay at a rehab facility, or making an appointment for private psychotherapy. Whatever your first step is, it's the willingness, desire, and intent you bring to it that makes movement possible.

The most constructive attitude to embrace during the forthcoming stage of movement is one of my favorite 12-step slogans: "One day at a time." Stay in the manageable framework of 24 hours and don't obsess about tomorrow, next week, or next year. Remember that each of us has only the present moment at hand. You will get "there" one step at a time.

Stage Three: Movement

The time has arrived for you to move across the bridge, beyond the first step. You've contemplated change, reflected on your past, and formed your intent. Now comes the stage where the inner work you've accomplished in the first two stages comes to fruition. You're the conductor of change in your life. You're now ready to progress.

As you place one foot in front of the other, resolve to keep going, no matter what happens. You're bound to meet some obstacles while moving ahead because that's the nature of change and of life itself. Remember, if we do not encounter hurdles, we're unlikely to grow. Instead of looking at these as blockages, consider them as invitations to fortify your determination to keep moving forward. Depend upon your inner resources to surmount these. Do not lose hope or despair!

Although adjustment after transition is not one of the three stages of transformation, I include it here because it naturally occurs after the necessary steps are taken. This is the time when we assimilate the new thoughts and way of life obtained from crossing the bridge into a new consciousness. This phase can take weeks, months, or years, depending on our personal circumstances, the nature of the change, resources available, the amount of effort required in undergoing transformation, and our physical and mental health.

Much like the previous three stages, this timeframe requires trust, determination, inner strength, and courage. It's also when we are most vulnerable to giving up and to entertaining hopelessness. Awareness is key to avoiding these pitfalls. Take your time and know that you are not in a competition to arrive at a set destination. You may fall backwards, but that doesn't signal defeat. Reflect on your courage when you initially crossed the bridge, remain hopeful and trust the process!

My Transformative Journey into Meditation and Higher Consciousness

My personal experiences of learning a meditative practice involve one of the most common issues people have struggled with during mediumship and spiritual development workshops that I've taught. As stated earlier, the most common complaint I hear regarding meditation is the inability to stop one's thoughts during the period of stillness. I, too, had problems with this in the beginning until I discovered that the goal was not to "stop" thoughts. In other words, the mind's inherent function is to think, so attempting to stop this mental process is futile. Instead, bring your mind along in your meditation journey and allow it to do what it does, with one distinct difference: *observing* your thoughts but not attaching to them. Placing distance between you and your thoughts in this way disallows your identification with them and the resulting spiral that they can create.

For example, during your meditation, you may have thoughts about the chores you have to do that day or an important work meeting on your schedule. Acknowledge these thoughts as they pop up by simply observing them. Allow them to fade out then return your focus to your breath (which will bring you back to the soul-consciousness space between thoughts). The worst approach to take is to wrestle with the mind because you will always lose. You will then feel discouraged, frustrated, and want to quit. By surrendering to thoughts as they arise, you can more easily detach from them.

Employ the power of observation. The purpose of meditation is to become aware of the higher consciousness of the soul, not the dissolution of all thoughts. Importantly, do not buy into the notion that you're not with the practice because you cannot shut down your mind. That's not the way it works.

One of my favorite analogies about thoughts is imagining myself sitting on a beach observing the tide. I am aware of waves as they flow towards me and recede from the beach. The waves are like my thoughts, ebbing and flowing in their own rhythm. Try this yourself in your meditation for five minutes or longer.

When I began my spiritual development during my mid-30s, I was eager to explore beneath the surface of my mind and personality to probe the depths of my soul. Although I had read numerous books on various metaphysical topics and obtained sobriety in a 12-step program, I had not yet stepped onto the bridge of engaging with my soul in a meaningful, profound way. During this period, I felt that there was something more that I had to experience in regards to my commitment to remain sober and grow spiritually. This compelling desire arose organically in me, and was the stimulating factor that drove me to read, learn, and experience all I could. I embarked on this quest with a fierce determination to grow.

Soon, I began to take various workshops at the Universal Life Healing Center in my hometown. I learned reiki healing, therapeutic touch, the basics of intuition, among others. One of the primary "activities" mentioned in all of these courses was meditation — something I had never done. Growing up in traditional religion, the church encouraged members to pray, but never mentioned meditation. Therefore, I had no preconceived notions about it, but knew I needed to do it to heighten soul awareness as never before. *What would I find through meditating? What if I couldn't "do" it?* I didn't know, but I surely wanted to find out and so I set the intention to practice it.

At first, it went well. The metaphysical center offered group meditations with guided imagery led by one of the ministers. I was able to still my mind for brief periods and connect with bits of the higher consciousness I so desired. Soon, I committed to a daily practice at home. I'd eat supper, do the dishes, and then immediately retreat to a spare room that I had dedicated to my spiritual practice. In those early days, I'd spend a full hour each evening in meditation. I bought CDs to accompany my practice and (hopefully) lead me into deeper states of consciousness. I rarely missed a day. If I did, I didn't feel balanced. Things went along smoothly until I hit a wall, constructed from my own doubts about what I thought I *should* perceive during these quiet times. Let me explain:

In my enthusiasm to develop the inner sense of clairvoyance, I believed that I needed to perceive images, spirit guides, angels, and the spirit world during meditation. When this didn't happen over the course of several months, I became discouraged and ready to give up. (As I noted earlier, patience is one of my lessons in this life.) I also falsely believed that I needed to empty my mind of all thoughts. No matter how hard I tried, thoughts popped in.

Frustrated, I began to skip this daily practice. In the beginning, I didn't realize that the real purpose of meditation is to transcend the thinking mind and connect with the higher consciousness of the soul. I believed that there was a *goal* to the practice, when the very opposite is true. I shared my discontent with others at the center until one of them informed me that it's impossible to fail at meditation and to simply let go of what I believed I should be seeing.

"You may not see, but sensing is just as important," a friend told me.

"You may not see your spirit guides, but you will build a stronger connection with them," another commented.

Encouraged by this advice, I enthusiastically resumed my daily practice. I had stepped onto the bridge of transformation and knew I had to keep moving. I wanted to reach for the highest spiritual experience possible.

Within a year, I began to offer spiritual readings at a metaphysical bookstore in Pittsburgh. Clients from all walks of life came to see me but I still felt as if there was more of the bridge to traverse.

One day, I was inspired to do a brief meditation before doing each client reading. After a while of doing so, I noticed that I felt more attuned to my clients — specifically, to their energy fields and their loved ones in spirit. From that time forward, I continued to meditate briefly before every private reading I gave and still do today. These brief doses of stillness eventually took the place of the hour-long meditations I had been doing previously. They make it possible to give my best to clients during sessions and are an essential part of my mediumship practice. These short periods of stillness connect me to my spirit mind, the domain of the soul.

As you can see, my journey across the bridge was initiated by the promptings of my soul. My desire for intimacy with my soul urged me to step onto the bridge. Along the way, my doubts and false beliefs nearly stopped the journey but were overcome by accepting helpful advice from fellow travelers. I stood up, brushed myself off and began again. My zest to experience higher consciousness nourished me throughout. I knew that I needed to stay the course and not allow my impatience to sideline me, as it had so many times prior.

By no means am I an expert meditator, nor do I think I will ever reach the consciousness level of Jesus or the Buddha — at least not in this lifetime. But I am doing the best I can and that is all that really matters in the end. This is true for you also.

Alexa's Journey of Transformation

The following story is an example of spiritual transformation motivated by both intrinsic and extrinsic factors. In it, you will recognize the three stages of transformation discussed earlier. Alexa's journey is particularly significant because of the stark contrast between her background in rational, scientific training, and her subsequent intuitive development. I share this with you to show how Spirit is ready and willing to meet and work with us wherever we may be on our unique paths.

I've had the pleasure of knowing Alexa, a medical doctor in her late 50s, since she first came to me for readings years ago. She's one of the kindest, most caring and compassionate people I've encountered. The first time we met, she and her mother came to my office for a session. Although I do not recall the specifics of the readings (I rarely do), she later told me how much the sessions helped both of them. Over the years, Alexa continued to connect with me for many life guidance readings and has referred multiple people to me.

One day, I asked her about her background regarding spirituality. Alexa's Lebanese family practiced devout Catholicism (in her word, "strict") and encouraged her to follow this religion and pray to God. Surprisingly, they also engaged in mystical practices such as reading coffee grounds and telling fortunes, although this was kept private. But Alexa was never encouraged to develop her own connection with higher consciousness or hone her intuition; instead, she was told to not waiver from the doctrines and dogma of the church.

Alexa spent years learning scientific data and methods in her studies to become a doctor. The combination of these rationally-based systems didn't deter her, however, from eventually searching beyond them for the spiritual dimension of her being. She shared with me that things dramatically changed for her when she took my workshop on the akashic files. Just six months prior to this, her husband had left her for another woman and filed for divorce. This was the first of several painful wakeup calls she was to endure.

"I was devastated. During times of trauma, you realize that you need to reach out to someone or some guidance from God to help you get through it. My prayer was answered when I came to your workshop," she explained.

During the group session, Alexa had a profound vision of one of her previous incarnations that gave her remarkable insight into the present-day relationship with her ex-husband. "It was a personal, mind-blowing experience, and now, of course, it's faded into the recesses of memory, but it's still very vivid in many respects, particularly regarding the emotions I felt during the meditation," she shared. "I gained insight about why the relationship took the course it did."

Alexa had two romantic relationships after her divorce, both ending within a relatively short time. These compounded the feelings of failure she experienced about her divorce. Following these breakups, as she sought my guidance, her spirit team and mine advised her to pursue her own spiritual fulfillment, apart from relationships. They acknowledged her feelings of inferiority and inadequacy in regard to relationships, but to not give those beliefs validity. Alexa had all she needed within; the relationships were teaching mirrors, reflecting her own perceptions regarding her self-worth. Of course, this was a false belief, but as with many people, the belief led to painful experiences and provided the opportunity to transform. She could now use these for self-exploration and growth.

Yet another wakeup call came when Alexa's mother (for whom she had cared) passed with severe dementia. One night, her mother connected with Alexa during a dream visitation. As Alexa described it, her mother was young and beautiful again with no signs of the dementia that had stolen her ability to function and communicate before her death. Her mother wore the same shimmery, blue dress that she was buried in. She was radiant and vibrant, as she had been before her illness.

"I remember you told me that we become young again in the spirit world," Alexa recalled. "That is how I knew it was a real connection. Attending your workshop and the dream of my mom gave me a taste of something much larger than the scientific training I'd had. I knew there was another dimension to life. My eyes were opened and I thought, *Why can't I do this?* I may not have the depth of skill you and others have, Carole, but surely I must have *something*. These experiences encouraged me to explore more and to continue to expand my spiritual consciousness."

Over time, Alexa became fascinated with all things metaphysical: intuition, mediumship, reincarnation, hands-on healing modalities, and even extraterrestrial life. I lost touch with her periodically due to her demanding schedule. Somehow, I knew we'd meet again.

The following year, we met for lunch and she asked me to mentor her in methods to sense higher consciousness. Until this point, I had only taught this in a group setting, but I was honored that she trusted me to privately tutor her.

"I want to have what you have," she shared. "I don't know how to attain that level of sensing. Teach me."

Not long after, we set up a series of Zoom sessions. In the first module, I asked her what she specifically needed help with so I could zero in on what would best meet her needs.

"I don't know. Teach me," she repeated.

I dug out notes and curricula for workshops that I had previously taught at Lilydale, and through my own practice, to gather some ideas. I also consulted with my spirit team about what would be most beneficial. They inspired me to teach Alexa the basics, beginning with simple mindfulness practices, followed by descriptions of the inner senses, enlivening the imagination to open the right brain, perceiving energy flow through the chakra system, and providing encouragement for her to trust her own intuitive perceptions. Each session was structured as an exercise that would naturally unfold her ability to perceive the nonphysical world of energy. The team made me aware that Alexa struggled with trusting her perceptions, and that this needed to be addressed. This, they said, could be accomplished through repetition of the exercises, feedback from me, and gentle reinforcement.

As the sessions progressed, Alexa became more open and trusting of her intuitive experiences. Alexa's journey across the bridge to heightened spiritual consciousness continues, and we still meet regularly. As a bonus, the sessions have helped me learn more about my own personal journey of higher consciousness because they fortified and refreshed me on the important basics of intuitive development. I was reminded that I can always sharpen my sensitivity through higher-sense perceptions. We're all endlessly evolving towards our genuine identity of Spirit.

Write About Your Personal Journey

Bring to mind a transformation you've made in life or one you anticipate making. If you have not yet stepped onto the bridge of transformation, imagine what your journey would entail during the exercise. This does not have to be something painful; it can be a welcome change that you're anticipating or one you've already made.

On a piece of paper, write a short title for your journey. Then list what the journey consisted of or what you anticipate, including circumstances present at the time, your feelings before stepping onto the bridge of transformation, and your reflections about what qualities you chose to bring along or leave behind. Recall what it felt like to step onto the bridge and feelings that arose during the transition.

Finally, write a few sentences about what adjustments were made when you reached the other side of the bridge. Is there more work to do? List a few steps you can take for further adjustment in your new space.

5

Dark Nights: Finding Meaning, Value and Purpose in Difficulties

Everybody cries and everybody hurts sometimes.
Hold on, hold on, hold on...
~ R.E.M.

"I can't see my way clear after my divorce," says Kim, 51, during a session. "It's been six months since the divorce was finalized and I have no clue about what I should do next. I mean, I still have my job, but other than that, my life feels empty. I'm depressed. All I think about is what went wrong in the marriage. My husband never opened up to me. I'm hurt, confused, and don't know where to turn."

I tune into the life force of Kim's soul. I sense depletion, emotional exhaustion, grief, and hopelessness. It's clear that she hasn't yet begun her journey across the bridge to a new way of being. A clairvoyant image pops into my mind of her standing knee deep in mud, crying, desperate to be released from the quagmire that traps her. I describe the scene to her.

"Yep, that's exactly how I feel!" she interjects before I've finished the description. "I barely have the energy to get out of bed. I feel as if I'm walking in sludge."

"What you're feeling is what human beings have felt for eons when a familiar way of life ends. Some have called this the dark night of the soul, a time when someone or something exits your life. It's a period of confusion, perhaps abandonment, and loneliness. You might feel as if God is not hearing you or is absent, hard to reach. Many of us feel this way when life suddenly changes, usually due to a loss," I explain.

"I feel as if I'm dying!" Kim exclaims. "I still have my kids but the family will never be the same now. Last night in bed, I thought about how empty the holidays will be without our family being together. I couldn't get those thoughts out of mind and was awake most of the night. What can I do?"

"The first thing is to let those painful feelings come up, no matter how uncomfortable they are. It does no good to suppress them. Feel the pain. But know that what you are going through is not forever. Feelings are temporary and mutable. Let's talk about the spiritual tools you can use to get through this."

My spirit team impresses on me that Kim's thoughts often center on the past and future. This, they say, is one of the first things she needs to change to avoid slipping into further anxiety and depression. I coach her in the practice of mindfulness to help her move her thoughts into present time. She explains that she can't focus long enough to do these practices.

"Start slowly, two or three minutes at a time, and place your attention on your breath. This is the foundation. Do this throughout the day. Even if you don't feel like it, make time for it anyway. Your breath is the vehicle that will transport you to the sacred sanctuary of peace within."

The session continues with encouraging messages from her spirit team about drawing upon her strengths, seeking support in counseling, connecting with nature, and other resources. Before the session ends, I'm impressed to pass along a message to Kim, one that my team imparted to me long ago: *This, too, shall pass.* And it always does.

Indicators of a Dark Night

What is the dark night of the soul? You've likely heard this term before but may not have personally experienced it. Yet. Be assured if you haven't gone through it, you most likely will at some point. Few things are guaranteed in life, but the loss of someone or something dear to you is certain. Relationships end, jobs are lost, illness occurs, old age creeps in, and death will come. Physical life and all that it entails are temporary conditions; therefore, change and loss are inevitable. This is when we are most likely to experience a dark night and feel disconnected (perhaps abandoned) by God. Something or someone we've cared about, depended upon, cherished, or grew accustomed to has now changed or left us.

The experience of the dark night of the soul was first described by 16th century Spanish mystic and poet St. John of the Cross. Likely written when he was imprisoned, the poem (which John did not title) reflects the author's mystical journey to God, his desperation, his surrender to divine will, and intense desire for unification with God. His writings mirror the common human experience of grasping for hope and faith in the midst of difficult times. The theme of the poem is the necessity of surrendering to the higher will of God as the only solution for the alleviation of suffering. By doing so, the soul is purified of self-centered desires and at peace in its union with the Creator.[1]

Characteristics of these harrowing periods include feeling that life is meaninglessness, hopeless, and that reality has collapsed. We may engage in self-pity, feel anxiety or depression, withdraw from others and, in severe cases, have suicidal thoughts. There's no timeframe for the dark night since our unique ability to navigate it determines its duration. Some people emerge from it relatively quickly; others spend months or years in it. This period of anguish worsens when people become stuck in what 12-step programs call "stinking thinking" (negative self-talk). In other words, individuals' current states of consciousness determine when they will emerge from the dark. To help you through the process, counseling therapy, prayer, meditation, appropriate medication, journal writing, physical exercise, and volunteering/helping others are useful.

The most critical point to realize while in the dark night is that it's entirely our choice to remain disempowered by it or to instead allow the darkness to awaken us and, ultimately, *rebirth* us. Through the insights I've gleaned during contact with the spirit world, it's preferable to use these times to engage in introspection and strengthening our spiritual connection because that is the natural course of the soul's evolution. If that path isn't taken, the issues will arise again, at one time or another. Multiple souls in spirit have communicated to me that they've had to face, examine, and heal that which they didn't during physical life. We can learn from these communications that it's better to face this sobering time sooner rather than later.

Why do dark nights occur in the first place? In some instances, they come about due to our attachment to people, things, and external circumstances. For instance, I've read numerous accounts of well-known people — celebrities, wealthy tycoons, and politicians — who became extremely distraught when their loss of status, fame, beauty, money, or power occurred. Some became addicted to drugs, filed for bankruptcy, became reclusive, sunk into depression or, sadly, took their own lives.

In recent years, I've observed an uptick in suicides among young people who were self-described "social media influencers." A sudden rise in notoriety, followed by the loss of it, are very difficult for most people to cope with, especially those who are not psychologically or spiritually equipped to endure it. Many people feel as if they are nothing without external validation. This is the danger of having a strong attachment to the outside world.

In the course of a lifetime, the loss of people whom we love, and the deterioration of the physical body naturally occur. Preparing for these inevitabilities through spiritual fortification helps in coping with the dark nights that accompany them. As I've shared in my previous books, people who are spiritually grounded have a smoother pathway when grieving the death of loved ones because they rely on the internal, solid, eternal foundation of Spirit, which is forever present. Loss is not easy by any means, but those who are sustained and nourished by a spiritual awareness are less susceptible to depression, anxiety, and hopelessness.

Surrendering to Your Dark Night

As difficult as it may be, acceptance of loss, grieving, and acknowledging our feelings during the process enables us to move forward. Although it appears counterintuitive, surrendering to all of these is precisely what will propel us onto the bridge of transformation.

Contrarily, resisting them keeps us despondent and stuck. Living in the past, wishing things were different, obsessing over what went wrong, focusing on regret, entertaining guilt, becoming hopeless, and replaying negative thoughts are indicators of resistance. Consider the analogy of excruciating pain caused by a muscle that contracts in spasms versus the calming relief experienced when it releases and relaxes. This is how easing into acceptance helps to alleviate the pain that results from fighting against existing circumstances in life. It empowers us to take inventory of our options and ultimately begin anew.

In my life, I've had several dark nights — the most life-transforming one being recovery from addiction to alcohol, as I shared earlier. Unlike others whom I've met in recovery, I did not drink for decades, lose my family, or end up in jail or a mental health facility. But from the start, I couldn't handle alcohol and its disastrous effects on my emotional and mental health.

In *The Big Book of Alcoholics Anonymous*, it's stated that some people are naturally allergic to alcohol.[2] I know I am one of them. Given my behavior, I'm certain anyone who knew me then would agree.

The time came when I surrendered to the fact that I simply could not persist in the way I was living. Shortly thereafter, I took the first step of the 12 steps: admitting that I was powerless over alcohol and that my life had become unmanageable. Surrendering enabled me to break down the thick walls of denial I had built in order to continue drinking to excess. Burned out, exhausted, miserable, and emotionally destitute, I entered private counseling and began to attend 12-step meetings regularly. After a brief relapse, I've managed to stay sober through these resources.

I've always believed that the first 12-step recovery program founded by Bill Wilson (known as Bill W.) and Robert Smith (known as Dr. Bob) was orchestrated by Spirit. There's little chance that the 12 steps to recovery and maintenance of it could have originated from rational thinking. When I initially read the 12 steps many years ago, I felt them in the core of my being. They are spiritually empowering because they place sobriety in the hands of a power greater than the rational mind. Clearly, it is a transformative program that provides immeasurable rewards to those who earnestly follow it. In my case, it did nothing less than save my life.

The point in sharing my personal story is that if I hadn't surrendered and acknowledged my situation exactly as it was — with all of its accompanying misery and unhappiness — I wouldn't have stepped onto the bridge of change. You've undoubtedly heard the saying "hitting rock bottom." Indeed, that is what it feels like: stark, pitiless, hard-cold reality smacking us in the face.

Reframing Past Experiences

Surrendering means that we admit we've hit bottom and can't solve the problem through our own thinking or willpower. It means understanding that our personality and ego don't see the Big Picture, as much as we'd like to believe so. Importantly, it means that we retain the strength to reach for the higher perspective of the soul, which is capable of *reframing* dark nights as experiences in the journey of spiritual awakening. These experiences are essential catalysts to awakening spiritually.

What does it mean to *reframe* an event? Simply put, it's to view it through the panoramic vision of the soul. When I reflect on those past days of drinking, I've come to view them as necessary on the journey of gaining higher awareness from my soul. This is not to say I never look upon them with regret about people I'd hurt, opportunities I missed, or time and money I wasted. At times, I fell into the trap of remorse long after I'd made amends, worked the steps, examined my shortcomings, and carried the message to others who are addicted. Yet, I know I have given the one thing required to progress: my best effort. This is what you, too, can give.

Reframing an event or circumstance is a shift in perception from feeling defeated to viewing the event as one in millions that our soul has and will experience. By embracing this perspective, the circumstance does not define you because you do not identify with it. You place distance between your core self and the experience; in doing so, it becomes feasible to untie the knots of emotional pain you may feel, alleviate catastrophic thinking, gain clarity and consider your choices.

If you learn to view a hardship as one of many experiences that your soul has had in its unfolding journey of spiritual awakening, you will be able to place it in its proper perspective and lessen its weight. Your mind will not and cannot see it from that point of view but your soul assuredly can. This is the value of being spiritually grounded. Recovery and rejuvenation are then possible. Knowing in your heart that you are an immortal soul who will never die provides immeasurable comfort.

As inconceivable as it may sound, I have encountered many people who genuinely believe their lives are and will be *forever* defined by a traumatic event, circumstance or loss. Unable to move beyond the past, the trauma lives on in their consciousness.

There it controls all perceptions of life going forward. The shift in perspective hasn't yet dawned in their consciousness, or if it has, they've denied, ignored, or dismissed it. For instance, people who have had a bad childhood cling to those old wounds as an excuse to repeat unhealthy family-modeled patterns such as violence, infidelity, emotional divestment, or addiction. They take the easier, softer way (as "the Big Book" calls it) to avoid personal responsibility in life. Reframing is impossible when inner vision is obscured or absent.

An exception to reframing old wounds is Post Traumatic Stress Disorder (PTSD). In this serious condition, conscious control of past events usually cannot be accomplished without intervention such as psychotherapy, eye movement desensitization, and therapeutic drugs. The individual's nervous system, emotional responses, brain, and body are altered by severe trauma and are subsequently easily triggered by environmental stimuli. This type of trauma requires expert help in the rehabilitation process. However, some of the same psychological mechanisms are at work in this condition as in less debilitating ones: fear, anxiety, attachment to the past, catastrophizing, and mind monologue. The difference lies in the severity and duration of symptoms. If you suffer from PTSD, help is available through connecting with your local mental health facilities.

If you are in the midst of your own dark night as you read this, know that you are not alone. Realize that your pain is not who you are at your core. The event does not limit, diminish, or define you. Give your fear over to the calming presence of your soul. Prepare to be reborn!

Illusions and Disillusionment

"You'll love this movie!" my friend excitedly announced to me during a conversation about current movies. "From start to finish, everything about it is great," she raved. "The story keeps you on the edge of your seat and the characters are really interesting. I'm sure you'll agree once you watch it!"

The following week, I eagerly went to the theater to see the movie she had wholeheartedly recommended. Filled with anticipation, I quickly found a seat and awaited the start. Less than an hour later, I was irritated, restless, and bored. Not mildly bored, mind you. *Incredibly* bored, disappointed, and disenchanted by the shallow characters, pointless dialogue, and convoluted, implausible plot. I kept waiting for things to improve but they didn't. I optimistically searched for a redeeming quality about the movie and couldn't find anything. I couldn't wait for it to be over. I was the first one to exit the theater afterwards.

Being let down by a movie is relatively benign, yet it summarizes the same feeling of disappointment, discontentment, distress, and dejection that can be summed up in one word: *disillusionment*. Disillusionment is part of a dark night experience because it is harsh reality without the lens of rose-colored glasses. It's a sign that we may need help from others in order to understand why we feel as we do. At the very least, an extended period of disillusionment requires that we assess, examine, and question our thoughts and beliefs about what's led us to that point. What needs to change about our perceptions? Are they realistic or not? What can we change about our life or our perspective?

To understand what disillusionment means, we must first know what an *illusion* is: fantasies and distortions of people and things that we've conjured in our own minds, or those we've internalized that others have created. An example is an ad for a product that promises to provide security, popularity, good looks, or respect simply by using it. When we see an illusion of something, we do not perceive it as it exists in reality. Instead, we see it through the projections of what we want, need, or believe it to be.

During childhood, we have fantasies about various things that are not necessarily the way they truly are. When I was five years old, I was invited to be a guest on a local children's TV show that I regularly watched. Each week, at the conclusion of the show, the host would exit the stage by walking over a bridge with her dog by her side. On TV, the bridge appeared wonderfully magical with colorful swirls and glitter, leading into lush woods. Each time I watched the show, I'd wonder what was in those woods. Maybe fairies and elves? A gingerbread house? An enchanted village?

When I saw the bridge in "real time" and in person in the TV show studio, I was disappointed to discover that it was actually made of heavy cardboard connected to another cardboard backdrop (not into the woods) with orange electrical cords running beneath it! My illusions were shattered. How could it be this way when it appeared so alluring on TV? After that day, I never perceived the bridge on TV with the same awe.

When we're adults and we become disillusioned, it's helpful to consider that we've likely entertained unrealistic expectations about a person, relationship, place, or circumstance. Perhaps we hadn't taken the time to look beneath the surface, or we perceived only the positive qualities. Often, we want or need to believe things are a certain way in order to be congruent with the image we hold of them or how they *should* be. Thus, we avoid disappointment. Other times, we've failed to consider that others' experiences of people and events differ significantly from ours (such as my letdown in the movie theater). In many cases, neither individual is wrong; there's simply a difference in personal opinion.

Despite the depleting effects that disillusionment brings, it is frequently necessary for both personal change and spiritual awakening. It is the first sign that we're ready to move beyond unrealistic perspectives and embrace different ones. Or it indicates we're ultimately perceiving the truth of something we've been in denial about. In such cases, disillusionment is precisely what is needed to initiate a breakthrough.

Maybe we've placed someone on a pedestal, glamorized a career, believed we'd earn a promotion, or spent excessive money to obtain something we imagined would help us or improve our lives. Over time or suddenly, the idealized person falls from grace, the job drains the life out of us, or we accumulate debt chasing the ever-elusive dream of perfect beauty, a fairytale wedding or the ideal vacation. The fantasy has collapsed, withered, and died, replaced by feelings of regret, anger, meaninglessness, or boredom. But here's the good news about this time of disappointment: it can lead to greater self-knowledge, fresh opportunities, new friendships, and deep insights that spur us to make better choices and become more adaptable.

Things don't always turn out as we expect them to; that is the nature of life. The world is not designed to meet our personal expectations, and if we mistakenly believe so, we're sure to meet with harsh doses of disillusionment. How, then, can we use it to grow? Contemplate the following suggestions when disillusionment strikes:

- **Reconsider your perception** of people, events, and circumstances. What needs to change (if anything) about your perceptions? What steps can you take to improve these? If you feel burned out, consider taking a break to gain fresh perspective.
- **Check your expectations.** Are they realistic? For instance, everyone falls short of perfection. Did you project infallibility onto a person, relationship, or circumstance? Did you entertain the fantasy that no one makes mistakes? Did you mistakenly believe that your career would *always* be rewarding and exciting? Did you expect to instantly lose weight?

- **Assume a more realistic view** of whomever or whatever let you down. In the case of relationships, what are the positive aspects to it? Did you give too much weight to minor annoyances? Is the incident that disillusioned you singular or a pattern of behavior?
- **Accept that you are no different than others** when it comes to disillusionment. It happens to all of us and will probably occur multiple times during life.
- If you decide to move away from a person or situation, express gratitude for the relationship or experience. **Be thankful for the lessons**, keep those that benefit you, and let go of anger.

In summary, disillusionment is what you make of it. If used positively, it presents opportunities for healthy adjustments and significant change.

Below are true stories of courageous people who've navigated through dark nights.

Cathy's Dark Night: Surviving Cancer

I first met Cathy decades ago at a local 12-step recovery meeting. In the following years, we formed a close, enduring friendship that survives to this day. When I began professional mediumship work, Cathy often drove with me to group venues, helped design and maintain my website, offered helpful insights about the promotion of my work, and gave me encouragement when I was disheartened. After her move out of state years ago, we stayed in contact. Weeks passed between phone calls, but when we'd talk, time and distance were irrelevant to the bond we shared.

Over the years and through many changes in our personal lives, we continued to nurture our friendship. So, when Cathy informed me five years ago that she had been diagnosed with metastatic breast cancer, I was crushed. I unflinchingly offered my support as she was scheduled for surgery, chemotherapy, and radiation treatments in the next several months. I knew she had a challenging road ahead and I wanted to help her as much as possible.

Because the miles between us precluded in-person visits, I offered prayers, distance healing (reiki), short chats by phone, and greeting cards every week. Below is her story of navigating serious illness, crossing the bridge of spiritual transformation, and coming to terms with how her life changed.

"From the time I was young, I had faith in God," Cathy shared during a recent Zoom chat. "My family went to a Pentecostal church, but since then I've learned I don't have to be in a physical building to have God in my heart. Before the diagnosis, I was satisfied with my life. I had my own home, my friends, and a job. I felt comfortable with where I was in life.

"All that changed when I received a phone call one afternoon while out with a friend," she continued. "The way I found out I had cancer was especially shocking because a clinician from the hospital my doctor is affiliated with said he needed to schedule me for surgery without first explaining the results of X-rays that I had. But I had no prior communication from my doctor about this. Stunned by this news, I asked the clinician why I would need to have surgery. 'You have breast cancer,' he replied matter-of-factly.

"My first reaction was anger," Cathy shared. "I was angry that my doctor had not called me personally about the results of the recent mammogram. The call from the clinician stopped me dead in my tracks. It was a harsh way to learn I had cancer, but that's how it happened," she said, tearing up.

"When I confirmed the diagnosis with my doctor, I was still in disbelief. And then I felt profound sadness because I had witnessed my parents cope with having cancer. I didn't want chemotherapy or radiation. I didn't want to go through what they did. My family and friends had to persuade me to go through the treatments. I was angry with them, as strange as it sounds, because I felt they weren't in my shoes so had no right to advise me what to do with my body. I see now that my attitude came from feeling that I had no control over my life due to the disease. I was lashing out. There were many dark nights when I'd go to bed and think about what chemotherapy would do to my body. My thoughts also went to family members and friends who took the treatments and how sick it made them.

"After having surgery, undergoing the chemotherapy treatments was exhausting. Talk about a dark night! At times, I slept 18 hours daily. If it weren't for my friend who insisted I go out to eat with her, I would have stayed housebound the entire time. I was angry with God for putting me through this. I wanted to give up numerous times. If it weren't for my family and friends, I think I would have! And my aunt in spirit, who was like a mother to me, came to me several times during those days. One night, I perceived her whispering, 'You're going to make it, honey. You're stronger than you believe.' She had always supported me in life. Why wouldn't she now?

"I had to reach deeply into my soul to believe I would make it through the treatments. After the chemotherapy treatments ended, the radiation sessions began. In the months following, I developed neuropathy in my hands and feet. The pins and needles sensations were painful and interfered with my ability to work. But I was alive and the worst was behind me."

The day I spoke with her, Cathy was celebrating five years of being cancer free. I asked her how the journey had changed her.

"I no longer take life for granted. In the years since the treatments, I've felt as if I'm not confined in a dark cocoon anymore. I have emerged, transformed. I like helping people and showing them someone cares. The entire journey has brought me closer to God. I ask Him every day what He wants me to do on that day. I'm no longer angry at anyone. I don't do the blame game anymore. When I look back, I've learned that God is with me every day.

"The most profound lesson from surviving cancer is learning how to receive nurturing and care from others. I've been a giver all my life, sometimes to people who have shown no appreciation for it. I refused help for myself many times because I believed I didn't need, want, or deserve it. I was out of balance. During the dark night, I was forced to learn how to depend on others. I learned how to accept help just to get through every day. Through the illness, I believe God was telling me that it was now my time to receive the same care I had given to others. Today, when I rang the bell at the clinic to celebrate five years of being cancer free, I felt happiness and peace. It's truly a good day."

Joyce and Dan's Dark Night: The Loss of a Child

Joyce and Dan, husband and wife, contact me for a Zoom session. (Because I don't ask questions before a session, I know nothing about new clients and who they want to connect with in spirit. This has been my practice since the start and is vital to ensure purity of the session. I read from the blank slate upon which spirit communicators "write" their stories.)

Immediately after saying my prayer, I'm impressed by the presence of a young man in spirit, approximately 18 years old, who stands between Joyce and Dan (clairvoyantly) on my computer screen. I sense his lively personality and enthusiasm to communicate with them.

"I have a young man here who is anxious to talk with you," I begin. "Is this your son?"

"Yes!" they answer in unison. I notice that they both tear up.

"He's thrilled to connect with you and says he's with Grandma in spirit. This lady appears to have lovely salt-and-pepper hair, wears a full apron and is small in stature. She came to welcome him when he passed."

"That must be my mother from the description," Joyce responds. "She always loved him. I felt she was with him!"

"He impresses me he passed suddenly and that medical tests didn't reveal the cause," I continue.

"Yes, we don't know what happened to him. The doctor said he went over everything in the autopsy with no clear results. We're devastated and miss him so much," Dan replies.

The session continues with astonishing evidentiary messages from the couple's son who eagerly wants his parents to know he's still with the family and aware of current events. In one of the messages, he communicates knowledge of their current counseling sessions. Both Joyce and Dan affirm this.

"We've always been a close-knit family. Our two girls miss him terribly. We go to family counseling weekly to help us through this. I don't understand why God would take him from us. He was only 18! I've never been religious, but I always believed in God. Now I'm not so sure. Why would God take a young person? Do you have any insights about this?" Joyce asks.

I've been asked this same question by many others. It never becomes easier to respond since there's nothing I could possibly say that makes rational sense of such a tragedy. The only wisdom I can share is what I've learned from direct experience during thousands of sessions.

"It will never make sense to you on a rational level, but the soul determines the time of birth and death. Each is divinely timed, based on the unique needs of the soul. God does not 'take' souls. It is the soul itself that returns to its natural home in the spirit world when lessons here on the physical plane are finished.

"The best way to go on from here is to anchor yourself in spiritual awareness and comfort by finding the presence of Spirit within. Your son's death forced you onto the bridge of irrevocable change. It's something you didn't consciously ask for, but there's light at the end of the dark tunnel, even if you can't see it yet. If you can muster just a small amount of trust to connect with that place of stillness within, you'll keep moving through this one day at a time," I advise.

After this initial session, the two connect with me for three other sessions the following year. Each time, I witness their progression of personal transformation through transiting the dark night of grief. During the final session, Joyce smiles and laughs — the first time I see her do so. They make it clear (as I've witnessed with other grieving parents) that they'll never be the same but are committed to memorializing their son by creating a home altar dedicated to him, talking to others about him, and volunteering to help other parents in the midst of loss. Although some may not consider these activities to be particularly spiritual, they are nonetheless coping strategies that help to alleviate grief. If it makes people feel better and more connected to their loved ones in spirit, it's valuable.

There's no question that we'll all encounter a dark night at some point in life because it is part of our journey of being human. The way we handle this formidable time determines how much we evolve from it.

Embracing the tiniest glimmers of hope and trust lightens the burdens we carry across the bridge of transformation. As time passes, the glimmers transform into unshakeable trust in a higher order. We're not alone, not without grace, and certainly are not pawns in the hands of a harsh, uncaring god. Believe this and feel renewed purpose in each step.

Become the Observer of Your Dark Night

In your journal, write a few qualities you possess that will help you move through a difficult phase in life. Examples of these are determination, honesty, willingness, trust, and patience. Be still and feel each of these qualities within you. Imagine yourself exuding these qualities in the difficult situation. Feel this as deeply as you can.

If you are currently experiencing a dark night, write about the event that happened, your feelings in the beginning, steps you've taken to move across the bridge of transformation, and where you are today. Write from the perspective of the third person: "she" or "he" had this happen and did this or that. Don't fret about details; the important point is to become the observer of your journey, to see it from another angle.

Employ gut honesty in your writing. This is for you and no one else. When you're finished writing, read it. How does this objective perspective differ from your subjective (direct) experience? How are they the same? What steps can you take next in the journey?

6

Natural Laws, Personal Responsibility and Choice

It is not in the stars to hold our destiny but in ourselves.
~ *William Shakespeare*

"I don't know why I have so much trouble with relationships," Morgan remarks during a life guidance session. "I've helped many people over the years, and for some reason, they ditch me. After all I've done to help them, I never hear from them — not even a text or phone call. Can you tune in and see what is going on?" she asks.

I detect sadness, disappointment, and frustration in her voice. Her hurt speaks louder than her words. Morgan's spirit team steps forward to impress me with guidance about the quality of her thoughts, beliefs, and emotions concerning relationships. "Your spirit team points out that your thoughts about friendship need an upgrade. Some of your beliefs about relationships are the cause of your distress. For example, you believe the problem lies with others who don't appreciate or value you, when you undervalue yourself by overextension of your time and energy. Think about it: Are you helping others to prove how good you are, how selfless and giving you are, or are you helping out of genuine care? Are you trying to be a martyr?"

I sense that Morgan is taken aback by my questions. Timidly, she responds, "Well, um ... I don't feel it's me ... it's them! They are ungrateful. They use me. What does that have to do with my beliefs? How could it be me? I don't get it," she says, obviously flustered.

"Many of our beliefs and thoughts are subconscious — meaning, we aren't aware of them. We engage in self-sabotage until we recognize and change them. You can do that by becoming gut-honest about your motivations for wanting to help others. Also take a candid look at your expectations about relationships. You appear to think you must prove yourself to be worthy of friendship by continually giving. You don't believe you are enough without that. That's out of balance. We need to receive as well as give. Relationships are about give and take; they're always a mirror of us. If you don't believe you are worthy of others' friendships without playing the role of the giver, you will continue to attract those who take advantage of you."

Morgan is silent for a moment. "Okay. I don't see it, but I'm so tired of being let down, I'm willing to do what I must to change. What do you suggest I do?"

"Take some time to examine your experiences, thoughts, and beliefs about others. Are you trying to be a martyr? Do you need to be needed? Go back over the most recent experiences you've had and see what those patterns reveal. Recall how you interacted with others and their responses. You'll gain insight by doing this which is the top requirement for change. Once you do this, you can then adjust your thoughts to align with what you truly desire in relationships."

As the session ends, Morgan sounds much more hopeful and less resistant to looking within than at the start of our session. Months later, she emailed to tell me how much the guidance had helped her. She went through a period where she spent time alone reflecting on how she could adjust her beliefs and release expectations of others.

During that time, she realized that she was reenacting the roles that her mother and grandmother had played in relationships. These, she discovered, were roles of "giver" and "martyr" — just as her spirit team had pointed out during the session. She stated that she still didn't feel ready to make new friendships; that it would take time to build trust. Although still uncertain of what the next step will be, she expressed gratitude for her progress.

One of the most difficult challenges we face in life is that of going within to examine our responsibility for challenging circumstances that show up. Many people are averse to accepting this challenge because doing so requires rigorous honesty, deep introspection, and intense reflection about their deeply held thoughts and beliefs. On top of this, personal responsibility requires the stripping away of comfortable denials about our own contributions to circumstances. Yet without this personal examination, we are destined to shroud our real power by identifying as a victim, blaming others, and becoming a pawn in the hands of others. The abdication of personal responsibility works only until we are eventually forced to accept the fact that we are the masters of our own destiny. Yet we are never truly alone without the aid of higher guidance.

This chapter explores universal laws that we can align with to create the life we want. Depending on the choices we make, we are either going with the flow of higher spiritual truth (as set forth in the laws) or we are not. Discovering how these eternal principles energize and give manifestation to our thoughts also reveals how we can align with them to implement desired results in life.

The Seven Natural Laws

Since the beginning of time (whenever that may be), seven metaphysical, immutable, eternal principles have been the ultimate authority governing the consequences of human thought, behavior, and existence. These laws of nature function independently from human-made laws and *always* supersede them in precedence. Similar to physical laws such as gravity, Newton's Laws of Motion, Bernoulli's Principles, and Boyle's

Law, natural laws guarantee observable, identical effects and outcomes that result from specific conditions, causes, and input. In other words, A + B = C. When these elements (A + B) are combined, the result will always be the same (C).

Natural laws (as listed below) were documented in ancient Greek writings and were referenced in ancient Roman philosophy by Cicero. Both the Old and New Testaments make mention of the laws. During the Middle Ages, Christian philosophers Albert the Great and Thomas Aquinas wrote about the intrinsic, God-given laws of nature which govern the faculty of reasoning capability in humans, considered to be a divine attribute. Greek philosopher Plato believed that we live in an orderly universe and that humans need to live in harmony with that order. In his famous writing, *Republic,* he described the perfect community as one that lives in accordance with nature. In the modern era, both the United States Constitution and Bill of Rights are based on the doctrine of natural laws.[1] The right to life, liberty, and the pursuit of happiness are asserted as fundamental, inherent rights of all human beings.

Natural laws are impartial and nondiscriminatory. They are the manifestation of eternal, universal intelligence seeking energetic order and harmony in all of creation. They are the birthright of every soul, regardless of any external condition. Natural laws do *not* vary depending upon location, geography, nationality, religion, gender, or any other external condition. Their effects are not dependent upon or negated by the number of humans engaging in particular thoughts or behaviors; one or 1000 aligning with the law or violating it gives the same outcome. The expression, "What is right may not be popular and what is popular may not be right," sums up this principle.

It is possible to violate human-made laws and not violate natural laws because of the latter's supremacy and ultimate authority over all matters, regardless of human-made dictates. An example of this is found in local and state government laws prohibiting certain conditions, such as the legality of possessing certain weapons in one state and the illegality of possessing them in another. Another example is one state criminalizing the use and possession of certain drugs, and another decriminalizing them. In both of these cases, breaking human-made laws does not necessarily indicate natural laws have been violated. Unless weapons are used to kill (and not used in self-defense) or drugs are knowingly given to another to cause harm or death, no natural law has been violated. The inherent right to rule one's own body (including what is put into it) rules supreme. This includes the right to self-defense if one's life is threatened. We own our bodies and our lives.

The study and application of natural laws are fundamental to living a spiritually-centered, peaceful, balanced, harmonious life. Applying these laws brings immeasurable rewards, alleviates suffering, and quickens manifestation of our desires. Importantly, aligning with natural laws greatly reduces and eliminates the accumulation of "negative" karma which results from violation of the laws. The more aware we become of how our thoughts and behaviors correspond with these universal laws, the better we can transform them to live free of victimhood, fear, frustration, and disempowerment.

I discuss each law (in no particular order), include practical examples, and offer suggestions on how to apply them to your life. Note: You will undoubtedly notice that many of the laws overlap in their meaning. This is because they are related, intertwined, and bound cohesively to achieve harmony in creation.

The Law of Vibration

This law states that everything possesses a vibration or frequency of energy. Because thoughts are energy, each thought vibrates at a particular caliber. Using a scale of density, thoughts range from the low (dense) end to the high (light) end.

Thoughts of anger, fear, resentment, and hatred are relatively dense compared to the lighter ones of benevolence, gratitude, compassion, and love. This also applies to emotions, since all emotions stem from thought. Depending upon the quality of the thought, corresponding thoughts (energy) are naturally drawn to those that match their vibration or frequency. This law is sometimes referred to as the law of attraction. Similar or identical energies are attracted to one another; dissimilar ones repel. In terms of energy vibration, resonance means that two or more frequencies are similar or matching. Here's an example:

Diana desires to land a job where her talents are acknowledged, valued and respected. She's burned out, discouraged, and fed up with her current job where she's continually disrespected and underpaid. Yet she stays in the position. In order to attract her desired circumstance, her thoughts and beliefs must match what she desires. In order to do this, she must change her current mindset, which is undermining her ability to land such a job. When she examines her thoughts, she discovers that she is holding beliefs that she is not qualified, not talented enough, and therefore not worthy of a better position.

To anchor a new reality, she must change the self-depreciating thoughts to those of confidence, assuredness, and worthiness. By transforming these old beliefs and replacing them with self-affirming ones, she will align with the natural Law of Vibration, and a new, better job will manifest. Otherwise, she will continue to attract similar situations. We cannot continue to replay the same thoughts and expect different results. That is impossible due to this law.

You are no doubt familiar with the statement, "Our thoughts create our reality." This is true by virtue of the Law of Vibration, yet we must allow for the variables of time and the state of our own consciousness. Regarding time, the more we are aligned with the law, the quicker the manifestation. The less we are aligned (or not aligned at all), the longer it will take to see results in the physical world. In terms of consciousness, if we are ignorant of the law (we don't know it exists), our awareness must be raised to include knowledge of it. If this doesn't occur, the law(s) still function since they are independent of our personal awareness of them. On the other hand, knowledge of the law, but resistance to it, creates delays in manifestation, stagnation, and karma (which will subsequently need to be addressed). This may be called willful ignorance wherein we possess knowledge, but deliberately avoid applying it.

Applying the Law of Vibration: Because this law rules the ability to attract what we want in life and dispel what we don't, access the quality of your thoughts. Treat others as you would appreciate being treated (the golden rule). Align your thoughts with what you want to see in your life. Imagine your life as you want it to be. Remember that to "be" it, you first must "see" it. Follow this law closely and you will see for yourself how powerful your thoughts are in creating the life you want.

The Law of Relativity

Simply stated, this principle asserts that everything we experience is relative to something else. The meaning we ascribe to anything is based in comparison and contrast to something else. In other words, we define experiences and things based on their relationship to other experiences and things. This law is startlingly apparent in a multitude of contrasts we see in the physical world. In fact, nothing has meaning but that which we can compare it to. The duality of the physical dimension is a demonstration of this principle. Let's look at several examples of this law.

Jason earns $15 per hour working full-time in a US-based retail store in 2023. That amounts to a monthly wage of approximately $2500, minus taxes. For him, this wage is not enough to sustain his expenses of rent, utilities, car payments and food. In India, the average monthly income for a working individual in 2023 was $387. That level of income is below poverty level in the US. Comparatively speaking, a person in India earning Jason's salary would consider himself well off, perhaps even wealthy.

Another example is the comparison of skills among individuals. To someone who has mastered a particular skill, like playing the piano or rebuilding a car, that skill is easy. But to one who has no knowledge or practical experience of playing music or car mechanics, it is confusing and difficult. The Law of Relativity states that everything obtains meaning and relevance based on its vibration in comparison to everything above and below it.

This law also applies to size. For instance, Jessica lives in a modest, older home with two bedrooms and one bathroom. She considers her home small. By contrast, Matt lives in a one-room basement apartment in a large city. When he visits Jessica in her home, he remarks about how spacious the place is, even though she does not view it as such. This is an example of the Law of Relativity in practical terms.

Applying the Law of Relativity: This law permits us to consider multiple perspectives regarding a person, thing, event, or situation. It gives us the faculties of open-mindedness, fair assessment, and expanded understanding through comparison and contrast. By applying this law, we can look upon people and situations we encounter with greater depth and knowledge before unfairly judging them. Put this law into action by resisting the urge to make snap decisions and judgments. Open your mind to experiences beyond your own.

The Law of Cause and Effect

Every cause has an effect and vice versa. For every action, there is an equal and opposite reaction. This law may also be called the law of karma or "what goes around, comes around." The only variable is time, an artificial construct of physical reality. However, once a cause is set into motion, the effect is inevitable. On the physical plane, everything that manifests (effect) is the result of thought (cause). This is precisely why our thoughts are so powerful, even if we do not recognize this fact. Everything we see, hear, touch, smell, or taste on the physical plane originated with thought.

The founding of the United States was conceived (thought of) by a group of people who passionately envisioned a nation where the freedom principle (life, liberty, and the pursuit of happiness) was paramount and the inherent right of all human beings. This example also illustrates how the power of desire fuels manifestation. By aligning themselves with the principles set forth in natural laws, the founders established a sovereign nation, independent from autocratic rule. The group of founders fervently entrusted the creation and sustenance of the new nation to God. The Bill of Rights originated from thoughts about the rightful liberty for all citizens.

In metaphysical terms regarding the soul's journey throughout physical existences, qualities of souls' chosen personalities, skills, natural abilities, and even illness are the effects of thoughts held by souls across multiple physical lifetimes. Time is irrelevant since the soul is immortal. To cite an example, if a soul held thoughts of extreme, arrogant independence in one incarnation, it may return to earth as a person who needs constant care from others (perhaps as an invalid) to balance the extreme independence from the prior lifetime. This is also an example of the Law of Polarity discussed below. Extremes work together to modulate polarity.

Ingrained thought patterns from one's current lifetime are also causes which produce effects. Most people are not aware of what subconscious thoughts they've internalized from family, environment, and culture. Instead, they witness only the results that manifest from these hidden thought patterns. It takes courage and determination to dig deeply into oneself, pinpoint unbalanced thoughts, and transform them.

This process is sometimes referred to as "shadow work" and can involve psychotherapy, energy healing, or spiritual counseling. This inner-self-examination is similar to what is encountered in the dark night when we confront beliefs that have produced emotional turmoil, insecurity, confusion, anxiety, or depression. The difference is that the dark night is typically triggered by the loss of someone or something, whereas shadow work may arise in any circumstance. To successfully navigate either, fearlessness, honesty, and determination are necessary.

The Law of Cause and Effect is the only way that reality is created. There is no disorder or chance in the universe; however, disorder and chaos often precede change as necessary components of the transformative process. When change is accomplished, order is once again restored. This cycle is repeated multiple times throughout life. Understanding and working with this law is critical to living a successful, righteous life. This power lies within each of us. Using this law consistently brings happiness, compassion, peace, and true justice.

Applying the Law of Cause and Effect: The supremacy of this law in creating the lives we want cannot be overstated. To begin to apply it, first take an honest look at your thoughts about yourself, your life, others, and various circumstances. Use an example from your life where your thoughts (cause) produced desirable effects. Then think of an event where an undesirable outcome resulted from your thoughts (effect).

I suggest writing these down in order to gain clarity. For instance, imagine you have a healthy, long-term, satisfying relationship. What thoughts about yourself (self-image) and others produced the "effect" of the relationship? On the other end, perhaps you've experienced loneliness. What thoughts do you hold that might have created this condition (effect)?

Be mindful of your thoughts and your reactions to people and events. Weed the garden of your mind daily through meditation to ensure that those are the things you truly desire to grow and harvest in your life. Remember, if you don't want something, don't allow your thoughts to dwell upon it. Instead, imagine and focus on what you would like to experience in life. By way of example, focus on health and joy as opposed to pain in your body or sadness about what you don't have. Focus on appreciating good people and circumstances in your life instead of those you perceive as negative.

The Law of Polarity

Everything in the physical world has an equal opposite: hot and cold, dark and light, up and down, right and left. This law empowers us to see all angles of people and circumstances. Simply stated, the perspective with which we view someone or something matters. Polarities are two opposites on the same spectrum, both necessary.

It is our personal perception that determines how we act and what we create. When we see polarities, we can blend both sides to reach an agreement, solve problems, and invent new solutions. We can create a harmonious balance between two extremes. The Law of Polarity is closely related to the Law of Relativity since it requires us to have an expanded perspective in order to consider all angles. This requires stepping outside of our personal comfort zone to learn about and embrace something we haven't considered before.

Have you ever been perplexed in finding a solution to a problem? Maybe you've desired something but had no idea how to go about obtaining it. Perhaps you focused on finding the answer but didn't consider all sides of the issue. Or maybe you had a mental block that you needed to break through concerning a vexing situation. The Law of Polarity assures that the methods (or plan of action) to achieve our desires exists, even if we aren't aware of them at the time.

It may take effort and time to find the method, but if we remain aware, alert, and focused, that information becomes known to us — often in unexpected ways. This is where engaging intuition and open-mindedness are valuable because when we least expect it, the answer we search for flows to us through a flash of insight, something we see or read, or other people. A closed mind does not work with the Law of Polarity, but resists it. Creativity springs from the consideration of all perspectives in any given circumstance. At times, the answer we seek requires the opposite of what we think it should be. This is where paying close attention to intuitive guidance and synchronicity comes in. Here's an example using the polarities of sadness and happiness:

Imagine you experience deep grief over a loved one's death. You think about the loss of the loved one from your life and how empty you feel without them. On the spectrum of emotions, you are at the lower-end polarity (in terms of vibration) of sadness, grief, and perhaps depression. But what happens if you consider and embrace the opposite end of the spectrum: joy, appreciation, and gratitude for your loved one's life? What if you recall fond memories of times shared and your loved one's contribution to your life? What if you know beyond doubt that you will forever be connected to this loved one through the bond of love? Your emotions begin to lift and transform. You become grateful for the person's presence in your life. Please note that this does not mean to suppress or deny your feelings of grief, but rather to view them as part of the *whole* experience of loving and caring for another. Loss is an inevitable fact of life, but we do not have to become victims of it. We can choose to focus on all of the good aspects of relationships that we enjoyed and thus modulate our response to loss.

Another example of this law in action is the process of transformation itself. Think of the expression, "When one door closes, another opens." In order to change, we must make room for that change. That often necessitates letting go of the old to make way for the new. In the case of leaving an established career for a new one, you may feel sadness, anxiety, and fear about closing the door on what was familiar and comfortable, on one end of the spectrum. On the other end are excitement, fulfillment, and enthusiasm to begin fresh, embark on new adventures, and engage your creativity or employ new skills. By seeing both polarities, the process of change is made easier and less traumatic. Often, we are unable to see the destination of transformation, but if we align with the Law of Polarity, we can integrate disparate information to make the best choice.

Applying the Law of Polarity: When confronted with decisions and the need to change, take time to consider all angles of the situation. Don't allow yourself to become trapped on one end of the scale. Write down both positive and negative perspectives regarding the situation. Keep your mind open, use your intuition as a guide and be fair-minded.

The Law of Gestation

The Law of Gestation refers to the period of time required for something to come into physical form. Human pregnancy takes approximately nine months from the time of conception until birth. Likewise, the time to incubate an idea (such as a business or product) from conception to manifestation takes varying amounts of time, planning, nurturing, and constructive effort. A creative project requires investment of focus, planning, patience, and applied effort to come into being. This is a necessary stage of incubation that allows for nurturing and maturation of the seeds we've planted. The time we see the form appear is dependent on the quality of our consciousness during the process. We are not separate from the creation; we are the administrators of it. We give birth to it.

The more we align with the Law of Gestation and the other natural laws, the quicker we see results. The less we align or resist, the longer it takes for results to manifest. The more focused we are on the desired result, the faster that result appears. As stated before, the physical plane is the only dimension of consciousness where time is relevant. It simply does not exist in higher levels of being, such as the spirit world. In fact, thoughts (cause) manifest (result) instantly there because there is much less density in terms of vibration than in the physical world. Duality — a condition of the earth plane — is not present in the higher realms of Spirit. (There are varying levels of consciousness in the spirit world, but not the concept of contrast as we know it here.)

Think of what happens when you plant a seed. Contained within that kernel is everything needed for the plant to come into being and "live out" its pure potential. Yet unless the seed is properly grounded in soil, watered, fertilized, and given the right amount of sunlight, it will not come into fruition. As we know, plants take time to germinate and grow. Our ideas are the same. So, in this example, we might say the seed is the thought of what we want to bring into reality; the roots are our determination and plans to ground it in reality; the water and fertilizer are supportive thoughts, attitudes, and beliefs that combine to produce the desired manifestation of the original idea. The thriving plant and the fruit it bears are the end results.

Why do people often fail to bring their desires into reality? The answer is simple: they forget to nurture the seed of that desire. People become impatient, disbelieving, distrusting, and discouraged. These slow down or stop the process of manifestation. Imagine a plant "believing" that it will never grow or thrive. The planet would be bereft of plants if this were the case; but the plant "knows" it has everything within it to grow, given the proper nurturing from either nature or humans.

Keep in mind that most things worth having in life take time. This fact is difficult for many to comprehend in a modern society that relies and expects instant manifestation and gratification. It remains true, nonetheless, because natural laws operate independent of cultural expectations and technology. To realize the results of our desires, we must supply the essential ingredients to bring those results into form.

To start a business, for instance, one must have a plan, the foundation upon which the business is built. Importantly, this includes a mission statement of the intent that will sustain the business. Ideally, the mission statement should focus squarely on service to customers, clients, or patients. The intent of the mission statement is the guiding principle behind the entire operation. This must be followed by practical, realistic methods that support the mission's intent and build upon the foundation (plan) to create the structure of the business.

As time goes on, the gestation period of the business might include practical concerns such as securing office space, the creation of a website, lists of methods to attract clients, a company logo, advertising, and purchases of needed materials and equipment. As the "birth" of the business approaches, further preparation might be planning a launch celebration, a special introductory fee, or the distribution of business cards and flyers. As you can see, the gestation period takes time, dedication, determination, and patience; but the end result is well worth it.

Applying the Law of Gestation: What do you desire to create in your life? What idea do you choose to bring into form? This does not necessarily have to be a tangible thing; it can be a new quality you want to embrace, a move to a new location or a career change. Write this idea down. Then formulate a realistic plan that supports the realization of your desire and record that also. List steps you can take in the process. Create a mission statement or intention for your desire. List specifics about what you can do to move towards your goal.

As you accomplish these, place a checkmark next to each completed action plan. During the entire process, focus on your idea, your mission statement, and your plans to bring it into form with unwavering clarity, patience, determination, trust, and commitment. Lastly, celebrate the birth of your creation when it is realized.

The Law of Rhythm

This law decrees that everything in the universe flows in natural cycles and motion is perpetual. "Nothing is constant but change" describes this law. Things flow backwards and forward, in and out, up and down. This is most evident in the cycles of nature: day follows night, planets move in orbits, seasons change, ocean tides ebb and flow. Our breath is rhythmic; the inbreath naturally follows the outbreath. Waking and sleeping are also natural cycles that we experience in daily life. The cycle of life on the physical plane is the creation of form (birth) followed by dissolution of that form (death).

Our emotions are likewise cyclical; we experience both good and bad times in life. Everything in the physical dimension is impermanent. All things will someday deteriorate and pass away from the physical realm. In the midst of suffering, this law brings us hope that if we hold on, things will improve. Understanding this basic fact is paramount to accepting that we have control over our thoughts and actions concerning these natural cycles. Knowing that "This, too, shall pass" gives hope, resiliency, determination, and fortitude during the inevitable down times. Nothing is forever, except the existence of our soul, which is indestructible and eternal.

Hard times and life challenges are necessary for us to evolve spiritually. They build character, endurance, strength, and creativity. Joyous times are equally necessary in the cycle of life: the birth of a child, a loving partnership, supportive friendships, and career accomplishments are reasons to celebrate. Employing gratitude for simple things — a warm bed, good food, and a comfortable home — makes the difficult times easier by lightening our spirits.

In today's world, the naïve misconceptions that one should always be happy and that life circumstances need to be perfect are rampant. These are unrealistic outlooks that can easily spiral into anxiety, depression, victimhood, and hopelessness. The truth is life is a rhythmic dance, consisting of ups and downs, disappointments and celebrations, joy and sorrow, having and not having. By understanding that the current conditions of one's life can and will change by virtue of this natural law — either naturally or through applied efforts — engenders hope, patience, fortitude, and optimism.

Making personal efforts to change the current condition through transforming one's thoughts, beliefs, and actions help to quicken desired results. Of course, we can choose to work against the law by stubbornly clinging to the notion that "this" is the way it will always be. Because energy is impartial and responds to the input of our thoughts by producing more of the same (the Law of Vibration), we may very well not *allow* the temporary condition to pass through our own resistance. Let's look at an example.

Megan's husband passed two years ago. Although she has gone to psychotherapy and grief counseling, she describes herself as "stuck" in grief. She simply cannot get over losing him. If she could accept that death is a natural part of the rhythm of life (and not the end of it), she could then trust that her husband will continue to be connected to her through the eternal bond of love. He is not "gone"; he lives on in spirit, despite his physical absence.

Our souls make a relatively brief appearance here in the world of form and then return home to the spirit world. As stated earlier, knowledge of the natural cycles of birth, death, and the eternity of the soul is a healing aspect of mediumship. This is not to say grief should be suppressed or ignored, but rather recognized and accepted as a rhythm of the natural life cycle. We pass through numerous cycles on our physical journey, each equally important to our continuing evolution.

Applying the Law of Rhythm: When you look back on your life, what natural rhythms of life stand out? Recall what feelings you had during these cycles, how you coped with both good and bad times, and what the experiences revealed to you. What did you learn about yourself? About the nature of life? As you consider the cycles of your life, what would have happened if you had given in to the notion that circumstances would remain the same?

The Law of Transmutation

Much like the Law of Rhythm, this law asserts that universal energy is in perpetual motion, transformation, and never at rest. Because of this law, all of creation avoids stagnation and decay. Transmutation means transformation or change. Our thoughts are energy and, as such, are capable of changing their form from mental energy into physical form through the creative principle.

Transforming mental thoughts into form shapes our physical reality, manifests our desires, ensures our progression as a species, and helps us to achieve goals. This is the inherent, potential power humans possess, as Jesus stated in Matthew 17:20: "Truly I tell you, if you have faith as small as a mustard seed, you can say to this mountain, 'Move from here to there,' and it will move.' Nothing will be impossible for you."

Focus, determination and applied effort are required for our thoughts to shape and manifest into reality. The Law of Transmutation ensures that we are capable of changing circumstances and experiences in life if we desire. Timeframes for results will vary, but because of this law, change is guaranteed. This is another reason to avoid victim mentality, as everyone possesses equal access to this law. Change is *always* possible and will come about sooner or later. It can arise organically (from outside of ourselves) or from our own internal motivation. To use this law to our advantage, we must think about what changes we desire, practical methods to achieve those changes, and use motivation, determination, and persistence to enact these steps until the vision of what we desire is created.

Depending upon the quality of the mental energy exerted, the resulting form can be either positive or negative. It can be beneficial or degrading, since the law and energy are both impartial. To use an analogy: Data (input) entered into a computer is impartial and will automatically produce corresponding results based on that data (input = output). Although human beings are not machines, our brains are indeed "programmable" and operate much the same as computers. The thoughts we "enter" into our brains and subsequently focus on determine the quality of our behavior and of our life itself. The more consistent the thoughts, the quicker we see the outcomes of those thoughts.

What happens when thoughts are contradictory or lack clarity? For instance, Tracy wants to lose weight but works two jobs, takes care of her family, and has little time to exercise. Because of this, she makes excuses about why she can't lose weight, almost guaranteeing that she won't. For change to occur, she must focus on her desire, take steps like building time into her schedule to walk or go to the gym, perhaps change her diet, and focus on her motivation and determination to change her weight. This focus sends a clear signal to attract thoughts, actions, and circumstances that support the achievement of her desire.

It's important to remember that each goal we have requires attentiveness and nurturing individually. In life guidance sessions, clients sometimes state that they want to make multiple changes at the same time. It's wiser to embrace one change at a time to prevent becoming overwhelmed, confused, and burned out. Choose your goal, gather your motivation, focus squarely on what you want, and take the necessary steps to use the energy of your thoughts to create change.

Applying the Law of Transmutation: What changes do you desire? Whatever they may be, you already possess the potential to bring these into reality. Clearly state your goal, write it down, and list the resources you can access to make it real. What small steps that will cascade into larger ones can you accomplish daily?

Know that your will is one of the most valuable assets you can use in the realization of your dreams. State your intent and go for it!

Use the Natural Laws to Your Advantage Always

Reminder: Applying the seven natural laws of the universe will help guide you through difficult times because they are fundamental to harmonious, balanced living, and assured outcomes. These laws are gifts from the higher intelligence of Spirit and just principles to live by. They are yours through birthright.

Part Three

Your Unique Spiritual Adventure

Who am I? Many people will respond to this simple question with their name, their relationship to others ("I'm John's wife" or "Rose's son"), their job title or position ("I'm the manager" or "I'm a teacher"), or perhaps in broader terms such as "I'm a human being" or "I'm a Buddhist." While these are all valid answers, these responses define who one is through external conditions only. If all of these conditions are stripped away, who are you then? Do you cease to exist without them? What lies beneath these veneers?

This section invites you to explore beyond the customary identifications you've assumed throughout life to arrive at the heart of your being, which is Spirit. You will discover that you are far greater than you've been taught or may have believed yourself to be. You will learn that your immortal soul has infinite, unbridled intelligence, and plans the perfect lessons you'll need before birth. Although many of these lessons present difficulties and challenges, when you courageously confront them, you will harvest rich rewards that will leave lasting impressions on your soul.

In Part Three, you'll learn what soul pods are, how to identify which ones you connect with, and how to apply those qualities in meaningful service. You'll learn about the significance of your natal astrological birth chart as it applies to your soul's lessons, skills, and direction. Additionally, this section delves into archetypes, their qualities, and how they are expressed. In the final chapter, I've included simple exercises and meditations to connect with your innermost self, diminish mind chatter, and find peace. Most of all, you will discover that the choice to connect with the Light within is always available to you in each moment.

No one can take your place in Spirit's unfolding plan. Your unique life circumstances, whatever they may be, are needed in the world. Your life has meaning, purpose, and direction. On this leg of your journey, you'll realize the electrifying power within and how to access it anytime you wish. Get ready to soar!

7

The Astrological Birth Chart:
The Intentions of Your Soul

A child is born on that day and at that hour when the celestial rays are in mathematical harmony with his individual karma.

~ Sri Yukteswar

"I don't believe in astrology," Vince says emphatically during our brief conversation following a life guidance session that focused on his career. His comment comes in response to my suggestion that studying his birth chart will help him through multiple setbacks in his career. During the session, he is clearly frustrated, disillusioned, and dissatisfied with the direction his life is taking.

"Astrology is mumbo jumbo and has nothing to do with the real world," he asserts. "How can planets control us? It's junk science."

I take a deep breath and swallow my irritation. *How should I respond? No use in getting into an in-depth explanation about the movement of the planets and their relevance to human life,* I think. *He seems closed. Maybe a simple explanation will help him understand the value of analyzing his chart. Here goes:*

"The planets don't *make* us do anything. They simply reflect and are symbolic of various energies within us, moving back and forth during their transits of the various astrological signs. Studying astrology is valuable because it gives clues into how and when certain events may happen to us in life. It points to lessons we need to learn in order to grow. Astrology is a resource and language to understand the dynamics of life and our spiritual evolution as eternal souls." I hold my breath in anticipation of his response, which I'm almost certain will be negative.

"You mean it's not the silly stuff like the daily horoscopes I've read in the newspaper and online? Well, I suppose there's more to it than I thought. How could looking at my birth chart help me?"

I'm surprised, almost shocked, that Vince is open-minded enough to express interest in discussing the topic. I keep my response light. "By examining your natal chart, it's possible to see what skills, talents, assets, and challenges your soul had at birth. I sense you're out of alignment with what your soul came here to do. Looking at the current movement of the planets reveals the nature and timing of various events in your life. It can also reveal how you can cope with difficulties using your own innate resources."

"Okay," he says, sighing. "Let's give it a go. Schedule me for one of those sessions."

Vince's reaction to astrology is one I've encountered numerous times in the course of my career. Many people falsely believe astrology is limited to what they read in the daily horoscopes. While horoscopes can indeed be accurate, they are by no means the full scope of the astonishing insights that can be obtained by studying a person's natal chart. The daily horoscope is a glossy, TV-guide version of astrology compared to the full-length "movie" of the natal chart. It's a micro-glance at each particular astrological sign compared to a full-blown microscopic analysis of the entire birth chart's configuration.

Simply stated, astrology is symbolic of diverse facets of both divine and human consciousness. It reveals what makes us tick, what challenges us, what skills come naturally, and when certain events are more likely to occur. Viewing the planets' locations at the moment of one's birth — their sun sign, house placements, and the planets' movements during transits —

helps us to understand the evolution of our soul. Far from being junk science, astrology is an ancient art that offers penetrating insights about the soul's journey. It is the *language* of the soul.

Years ago, I became fascinated with astrology and yearned to study it to understand myself more deeply. So, I signed up for ongoing classes to learn the basics of the planets, the houses of the birth chart, and the spiritual significance of the practice. Little did I know at that time that it would eventually become one of my favorite and most effective methods for supporting my clients in their life guidance sessions. Today I continue to study the movement of the planets to understand my life, help clients to understand theirs, and gauge the flow of collective human consciousness. In this chapter, I share how the birth chart reveals the soul's evolutionary intentions before birth, karmic indicators, and potential gateways for spiritual growth.

In the beginning of my astrological studies, I was overwhelmed by the slew of information I had to memorize. The symbols for planets, their correlation with human consciousness, and the meaning of houses and the aspects (relationships) between planets was daunting to absorb. In addition to taking numerous classes, I've read countless books about the spiritual significance of planets, their placement in the birth chart, and their reflection of human qualities.

Below I discuss astrology in a relatable way to help you understand it in terms of the soul's evolution. This particular branch of astrology, Evolutionary Astrology (EA), was formulated by Jeffrey Wolf Green in 1977. It is concerned with the ongoing journey of souls, based on their desires in prior and present incarnations. Because Pluto and the lunar nodes are key placements in this type of astrology, I discuss these as they relate to the specific evolutionary intent and desires of souls. I also focus on the significance of Saturn because it is directly linked to karmic lessons of souls. Although it is not typically considered in EA, Saturn's placement by sign and house are crucial in understanding specific challenges you may encounter along the way.

I suggest pulling up a copy of your birth chart before reading this material. If you don't yet have a natal chart, you can create one at no cost on any of the reputable astrology websites like cafeastrology.com, astrology.com, astro.com, and astrologyking.com. As you read each of the sections below, locate the planet or lunar node in your chart and refer to its corresponding explanation on the website's pages for further insights.

Pluto Symbolizes the Soul's Evolutionary Intent

As the outermost planet in our solar system, Pluto's movement (also called a transit) through the 12 astrological signs is relatively slow. (Although astronomers have declassified Pluto as a planet, its significance in terms of consciousness remains unchanged.) First discovered in 1930, Pluto takes anywhere from 12 to 20 years for the dwarf planet to travel through one sign and approximately 248 years to travel through the entire zodiac. As I write this in late 2023, Pluto is finishing its transit through Capricorn and will begin its journey through Aquarius in 2024 (although it will spend a few months backing up (retrograding) into the late degrees of Capricorn in the fall of 2024).

In terms of human consciousness, Pluto symbolizes the God-Force, the primal life force, and the individual soul. It symbolizes the deep transformation that needs to take place for the soul to further evolve towards unity with God and the areas of one's life (depending on its sign and house placement) where intense scrutiny is required regarding what lies beneath the surface. Its placement in the birth chart represents qualities that are not supportive of and downright *toxic* to the progression of the soul's evolution.

Pluto wants nothing to do with surface investigations; its influence demands that we dig deeply, honestly, and feverishly into our darkest, hidden desires and what makes us tick, so to speak. As one of the planets that rules the sign of Scorpio (the other is Mars), its evolutionary purposes are to first expose the impurities that lurk in our psyche and, secondly, to purge ourselves of them. Its influence is relentless, intense, and transformative. Its spiritual value is *purification* during the soul's journey towards reunion with the Creator. The image of the phoenix rising from the ashes perfectly illustrates the essence of Pluto's power. The old must be extinguished, burned away, obliterated, to make way for the new to arise.

The raw power of Pluto is symbolic of both creative and destructive forces in creation. Because humans are part of creation, both of these forces naturally exist simultaneously within us. Pluto represents birth, death, and transformation. Evolving spiritually requires the destruction of outworn patterns, obsolete beliefs — specifically of separateness from God — and anything else that hinders spiritual growth. This process necessitates obliteration of the old forms of being that souls have taken on to give rise to the new ones. Thus, death (physically or metaphorically) gives birth to a new way of being. The soul is purified through this process.

Where Pluto is found in the birth chart (by sign and house) is where one will need to confront the shadow side of oneself. Shadow aspects refer to unconscious patterns of thought, beliefs, and behaviors from both past incarnations and the current life. Because these are held within the subconscious, we are frequently not aware of them, except for when they are mirrored to us by others and the external world. Even then, we may deny having them by projecting these same qualities onto others. *Psychological projection* is the work of the ego, which creates defensiveness in the interest of self-preservation. We do not see undesirable qualities in ourselves, but easily see these same (unclaimed) qualities in others. Sooner or later, we must delve beneath the surface of our conscious mind to discover the hidden, secretive parts of self. This is the work of Pluto.

The 12 signs in astrology are expressions and archetypes (deeply ingrained patterns of human consciousness) of various human qualities that exist within all of us. Each of the 12 houses refers to a different area of the human experience. An individual expresses all 12 archetypes in varying degrees, depending upon the individual's personality and state of spiritual consciousness. (For further study, the explanations of each sign and house can be found on the astrology websites mentioned earlier, or others.)

To determine the meaning of Pluto's placement in your chart, simply look at the sign and house that it's in. Study the area of life for that house and the qualities of the sign. For instance, if Pluto is in the first house at the moment of one's birth and in the sign of Virgo, this means the individual will need to purify herself (the first house correlates to the personality-self) of old self-images to evolve. This is because Virgo is associated with purification, humility, discernment, analysis, practicality, work, and service. In this example, arrogance, egocentric tendencies, and superiority complexes must be dissolved with this natal placement of Pluto.

Another interpretation of Pluto in Virgo in the first house is the need to purge oneself of self-criticism, inferiority complexes ("I'm not good enough"), or assuming the role of perpetual servant to others and ignoring one's own needs. Either of these interpretations can apply, depending on the unique soul. In any case, there will be multiple opportunities, lessons, events, and crises in the person's life to meet the requirements of Pluto.

It's important to note that because Pluto moves so slowly, an entire generation of souls will experience its placement in a particular sign (although houses will vary from person to person). A generation, spiritually speaking, is a group of souls who share the same evolutionary intent and desires, depending on the sign Pluto is moving through. This comes about from the group sharing similar karmic themes throughout time.

Let's continue our example of Pluto in Virgo. This generation, born during the late 1950s to the mid-1960s, has been concerned with spiritual lessons regarding natural health remedies, the value of work, ethical service to others, and self-improvement or personal development since this is the meaning of Virgo. To understand your generation's Plutonian focus, study the meaning of the sign that Pluto was in at your birth. To discover what area of your life Pluto wants you to purify, look to the house it occupies. This is the area of life where you will need to dig deeply in the process of self-discovery, make adjustments, and purge yourself of all that is no longer serving your growth.

Understanding the soul's intent when it came into the physical world (Pluto's placement in the chart) provides guidance about the soul's challenges, karma, and strengths. It provides insights into why we feel certain emotions, what skills come naturally, what areas in life present challenges, and what our soul desires to accomplish. This knowledge may also give clues to a meaningful career choice, service to others, and one's deepest desires. Additionally, it reveals where concentrated, intense effort must be applied to move beyond outworn, stagnant beliefs, attitudes, emotions, and behaviors.

Pluto has a compulsive, obsessive, determined quality to it that one can fall prey to if moderation isn't taken into consideration. As the life force itself, Pluto is indicative of the will of God in its purest form. If our personal will is not in alignment with this higher will, Pluto reveals (at times, ruthlessly) what is out of order and how to transform our personal will in order to blend it with higher will. The "job" of Pluto is to help us uncover our fears, rage, addictions (of any type), psychological imbalances, compulsions, and repetitive thoughts and actions so that we can address these and ultimately release them. Much like the festering of a wound occurs to bring impurities to the surface during physical healing, Pluto brings the impurities of our psyche to conscious awareness where they can be clearly seen, examined, adjusted, or released. After doing so, we are free to replace them with more spiritually-centered ones.

Many people who know nothing about astrology experience a compelling desire to transform some aspect of themselves at one time or another in life. One doesn't have to be familiar with astrology to experience a yearning to change, yet the basic knowledge of astrology can heighten the understanding and implications of profound transformation. As stated earlier, the urge to transform oneself is triggered from within (intrinsic) or through a form of crisis from the external world (extrinsic). At what time in life are we most apt to feel Pluto's effects? These promptings are much more likely to occur when Pluto forms a relationship with one of the personal planets (Sun, Moon, Mercury, Venus, or Mars) as it moves through the zodiac. During these times, it's beneficial to use one or several of the healing modalities mentioned below.

At this point, you might be wondering how you can follow the message of Pluto and what measures you can take to navigate the spiritual lessons it reveals. There are different avenues of healing that are valuable during the transformative process. Because of Pluto's close association with the psyche, private counseling can offer insights during the process. Journaling through introspection, energy healing, meditation, and gut honesty from others' feedback are likewise helpful. As much as it may hurt to examine the unbalanced parts of the self, we must take that plunge to grow. Importantly, the journey of Pluto's purification is slow and deliberate. It is not an overnight "one and done" to expose, examine, and release ingrained patterns! These certainly didn't form in a day and can only be released with focus, determination, persistence, and inner strength. Don't give in to the temptation of glossing over whatever arises since you will need to confront it again down the road — often in a very unpleasant manner. Take your time, focus on the positive attributes of yourself for a balanced assessment, and ask for guidance from your soul's wise perspective. Leave no stone unturned.

Considering that Pluto is symbolic of physical death in addition to psychological death, it brings lessons of grief and loss to the surface of our awareness to be emotionally processed. It is not uncommon for people to lose loved ones during significant Pluto transits. From the initial feelings of loss to the end stage of acceptance, the stages of grief take time and perspective for most people. This is evident in many mediumship sessions I've given. Old wounds from the relationship with the deceased, unresolved emotional business, and both loving and hurtful memories arise in the grieving process.

There is no set timeframe when one is healed or "over it." Yet by staying the course and allowing emotions to surface, you will move forward in the journey. During the process, it's helpful to focus on positive memories of your loved one. Cherished times, happy interactions, and significant, shared life events are treasures you'll retain forever. You may also consider how the relationship enriched you and what you learned about yourself from it. Give these memories their rightful place in your heart.

During personal transformation, imagine what your life would be like without the extra baggage of old patterns. Journal about what new thoughts will replace the old ones. List your positive behaviors, engage in gratitude, affirm your progress, and move forward one day at a time.

Saturn as Teacher

The sixth planet from the sun, Saturn is symbolic of the soul's karma, spiritual lessons that are incomplete or need to be reworked, and the areas of life in which the soul will meet tests and challenges. It represents maturity, wisdom, old age, time, discipline, responsibility, boundaries, limitations, effort, restrictions, justice, achievements, and rewards for applied effort as the soul journeys through physical life. In astrological parlance, Saturn is often referred to as the Lord of Karma. It's associated with all things physical, including the body. Its transit through each sign takes approximately 2.5 years and 28 to 29 years to travel through the entire zodiac.

Traditionally, Saturn has been considered a malefic influence by astrologers, yet this is not a fair assessment. In order to evolve in the schoolroom of earth, it's necessary to encounter, confront, and endure challenges and hardships. The familiar motto, "No pain, no gain," is indicative of the influence of Saturn. To grasp the implications of this, consider the events of your life that have been strong catalysts in your growth or those that contributed significantly and profoundly to your self-awareness. Chances are, these events were painful, difficult, or required concentrated effort on your behalf to push through them. This is the primary lesson of Saturn: to grow through the confrontation of challenges. It calls for us to create something enduring, lasting, and solid — either tangible or intangible — wherever it appears in the natal chart.

The sign and house placement of Saturn in the birth chart reveals where we're likely to struggle, meet obstacles, experience frustration, and face karma. Saturn's influence demands facing these challenges head on *without denial* to learn crucial lessons in life. The specific lessons and the means to master these depend on Saturn's location by sign and house at the time of birth. If we ignore its call to action, the lessons it brings become compounded, stronger, and harsher. It is always preferable to deal with Saturn earlier rather than later.

Saturn's association with justice is both earthly and karmic (spiritual). It rules the government, legal system, courts, and prisons, as well as the karmic principle and natural law of cause and effect. Although it is often viewed as punishing, difficult, harsh, and rigid, its actions are indisputably fair, *according to natural law*. One receives what one creates. Ignorance of the spiritual Law of Cause and Effect does not prevent its action; we will undoubtedly earn what we have put forth — good or bad — with no exceptions. The fact that we don't have conscious awareness of why certain events or circumstances occur does not mean we are not required to confront them. Rarely are we aware of prior lifetime karma, yet we are nonetheless responsible for all we've created through our thoughts, beliefs and actions. The location of Saturn by sign and house shows what we've created in prior incarnations and what must be confronted to further those lessons. It is not a "punishment," but an opportunity to grow.

You might wonder how Saturn provides rewards given its hard-nosed, critical nature. The answer is that when the required work in a specific area of life is accomplished, the reward follows. This certainly doesn't occur overnight; rather, it happens through time, persistence, and diligence. Saturn is the "corrector" of our lives with the intent of moving us forward spiritually through applied focus, effort, and determination. Then and only then can we claim mastery over a particular area of life.

To cite an example, imagine that Saturn sits in a birth chart in the sixth house in the sign of Libra. The sixth house is concerned with humble service, work, practicality, daily living, companion pets, detail, analysis, and mental processing. Libra is associated with relationships of all types, beauty, aesthetics, society, balance, equality, fairness, law, and courts. This individual will need to employ fairness, harmony, balance, and a service-oriented mindset in daily life and the work environment. He or she may feel a calling to work in some aspect of law, society, small animal care (veterinary work), or in beatifying environments, such as interior decorating. In any case, the qualities of Libra need to be embraced on a regular, consistent basis: fair-mindedness, others' needs (in addition to one's own), equality, and harmony. By meeting Saturn's requirements, karma is balanced and the qualities of the sign it occupies are accomplished. Each 28- to 29-year cycle of Saturn adds more experience to its lessons.

During karmic astrology sessions I've given, individuals often ask about their life purpose, if they're on the right track, and what they can do to align with a meaningful, happy life. In response to this, one of the placements in the chart that I consider is Saturn. This is due to the fact that if we are aligned with our soul's intent for life, we will undoubtedly reap rewards by doing the necessary work. Our greatest challenges often produce our deepest sense of fulfillment, although we rarely recognize it at the time. In some cases, mastery of these lessons opens us to the possibility of helping others who confront the very same issues. We've walked the path, done the work, and can therefore offer valuable insights to others. In the above example, the person with a sixth house Saturn placement may go on to volunteer at a homeless shelter (meeting the needs of society through selfless service), offer low-fee legal counseling, or work at a pet rescue shelter. Donating time and experience to those in need produces its own rich rewards and leads to deep, lasting fulfillment.

In addition to Saturn's role as a karmic indicator of new or unfinished lessons, its placement in the birth chart also relates to areas of life where certain lessons need to play out through more practical experience on our behalf. In other words, we may have dealt with the issues in prior lifetimes, but we need more real-time experience to "graduate." To illustrate this point, imagine that in a prior lifetime, a person was prevented from expressing herself creatively and uniquely. She may not have been considered an individual with her own thoughts and opinions in her native culture. She may have lived in a society that had strict gender roles in which women were not permitted to write, paint, or engage in creative pursuits outside of the domestic realm. So, while she did indeed create, it was in a very limited scope, such as utilitarian sewing for her family. This person entered her current life with an underdeveloped ability to create using her own faculties. In this case, Saturn may likely be situated in the fifth house (associated with creativity, the individual's unique personality, and expression). The sign it appears in indicates what flavor the creation will have; for example, if Saturn is in Sagittarius (spirituality, philosophy, religion, and foreign travel), she may write books about or take photos of sacred sites that she's traveled to in countries outside her own.

When working with this placement of natal Saturn, this person may find it difficult to aspire to her own subjective promptings to create something using her unique personal skills. Or she may feel that she, herself, is not of value and must work in the current life to recognize her inherent worth. By following her soul's promptings, she will meet the challenge of Saturn and reap the rewards of personal creativity.

I can't stress enough that the most crucial point to know about challenges, difficulties, and hardships is that through experiencing them, we gain strength, character, resiliency and fortitude. They are not present for punishment; they are in our lives to use for our personal evolution. We are not victims of fate, but masters of our destiny when we navigate hardships and learn through them. This is the ultimate reward of Saturn in all areas of life.

The Lunar Nodes

Unlike the planets, the lunar nodes do not have a solid form. We cannot look through a telescope and see them. Instead, they are mathematically calculated in a birth chart using the position of the natal moon in the chart. They are points where the moon's orbit around the earth intersects the ecliptic plane of the earth's orbit around the sun. Every planet has nodal points, but the lunar nodes are the ones most associated with the journey of the soul throughout time since the moon is symbolically associated with souls' past experiences.

For our purposes here, I will discuss their symbolic significance as they relate to both prior and current experiences of the soul. The nodes are of karmic importance in accessing souls' spiritual consciousness brought forward to the present life, as well as future lessons necessary for evolution. Their polarity works together to harmonize and modulate seemingly opposite perspectives of any experience. Through this blending, we evolve.

There are two specific nodes to consider: the south node and the north. They are directly across the zodiacal wheel from one another, occupying the same degree of opposite signs. For example, if one's south node is at 17 degrees in the sign of Cancer, the north node will be at 17 degrees Capricorn. (Cancer and Capricorn are directly opposite in the zodiac.) This is called the nodal axis or polarity. Some astrologers call the nodal axis the Axis of Fate since it is indicative of karma. Even though each of the 12 signs are opposed to another and appear to symbolize divergent qualities, they intertwine and operate as a single, whole, unified consciousness when they are blended, much like the Law of Polarity. I explain how this works in the sections below.

The sign and house placement of the nodes at birth reveal where we've been, what we've done in the past, and where we're going in the present life. They change signs in a backward motion (clockwise) approximately every 18 months. (By contrast, the planets move counterclockwise.) Studying the nodes helps us to comprehend not only our current spiritual lessons, but also recognize past, repetitive, familiar patterns of consciousness that we've held in prior incarnations. In terms of our individual consciousness, the south node shows the roots of current daily habits, attitudes, behaviors, and patterns of consciousness; the north node indicates the direction we're headed in for new growth potential. Past patterns do not necessarily have to be released but they can be used to move us forward in the experience of current lessons that our soul has intended before birth if we've incorporated the lessons from them into our consciousness.

People are naturally "pulled" to the qualities of their north node natal placement without conscious awareness of it. This draw is felt through inner promptings, intuitive nudges, affinities, and curiosity. For instance, I have always been fascinated with paranormal topics and psychology since childhood. Of course, I had no knowledge of astrology, much less the lunar nodes, in those days. Yet I was drawn to study and read as much as I could about these topics due to my north node's placement in the sign of Scorpio (the occult, metaphysics, death, rebirth, transformation, and psychology) in the third house (curiosity, the gathering of knowledge, communication, writing, and learning). As you can see, it was quite natural for me to take an avid interest in these areas, as I still do today.

The North Node: Current Life Lessons

The north node, by sign and house placement, reveals new or expanded lessons for the soul. Its location, by house and sign, reveals the soul's evolutionary intent prior to incarnation. The north node is also referred to as the Dragon's Head in astrological language because it represents the forward movement that the soul needs to take in its continuing growth. This node indicates where the soul needs to have either new or expanded experiences in the areas of life corresponding to the house and sign in which it appears. In the birth chart symbolism, this node appears in charts as an upside-down horseshoe.

When learning about the lessons of our north node, it's useful to assign an archetype and several general themes for the house it occupies. For instance, if the north node is in the ninth house, the archetype is the Student/Explorer, and the focus is on themes of travel (particularly internationally), as well as studies in higher education, learning, writing, and publishing. For your reference, I've listed these below, along with the positive expressions of each (as opposed to the "shadow," or unbalanced expressions). The soul will ultimately need to embrace these roles and qualities as part of its evolution.

As with all of the signs, there are both positive and negative expressions associated with the nodes. These are dependent on the free will/choice of the individual. An example of this is a north node located in the first house. Used positively, the person will need to embrace healthy self-esteem, independence, assertion, and courage. If expressed negatively, arrogance, extreme independence, aggression, and violence may be expressed. Moderation, flexibility, and balance are key to following the lessons of our north node.

- **House 1: The Assertive Self:** assertiveness, self-expression, courageousness, and independence.
- **House 2: The Resourceful Self:** acquisition, management and appreciation of material goods, real estate ownership, steady work, knowledge and appreciation of non-tangible values and inner security.
- **House 3: The Communicator/Writer:** communication of all types, gathering of facts and data, application of knowledge, writing, learning, and rational intelligence.
- **House 4: The Homebody:** home, family, ancestral roots, maternal instincts, and emotions.
- **House 5: The Unique Creator:** self-expression, creativity, children, and development of the unique personality.
- **House 6: The Hard Worker:** practicality, critical analysis, humble service, detail orientation, and problem solving.
- **House 7: The Partner:** diplomacy, equality, marriage, partnership, cooperation, and mediation.

- **House 8: The Deep Diver:** research, investigation, the occult, the mystical, transformation, psychology, and spirituality.
- **House 9: The Student/Explorer:** study, higher education, philosophy, publishing, and international travel.
- **House 10: The Administrator:** achievement, organization, leadership, public recognition, and management.
- **House 11: The Friend:** groups, organizations, humanitarianism, friendships, and social responsibility.
- **House 12: The Dreamer:** insight, intuition, meditation, dreams, the unseen realm, behind-the-scenes work, and privacy.

To further illustrate the influence of the nodal placement on souls' experiences, let's again consider the prior example of the north node's placement in the sign of Capricorn. This soul will be pulled to experiences and lessons of that sign: persistence, diligence, accomplishment, stability, achievement, administration, and the external world. These qualities may show up in various ways to give ample opportunity for the soul to experience and embrace them.

For instance, this person may be drawn to business ownership, management, or executive administration. He or she may live a life of prominence in the public eye, authority, leadership, or fame. Because the north node placement represents previously unexplored territory (or the need for expanded experience) in the house and sign it occupies, difficulties may arise due to unfamiliarity with these qualities. In this example, the person may have recurring feelings of inferiority, self-doubt, or work addiction in order to prove worthiness. These will need to be addressed and ultimately overcome. As experience is gained, the terrain of the north node becomes more familiar.

It's crucial to remember that just as the lessons of Saturn prompt us to surmount obstacles to gain mastery, the north node lessons bring opportunities and events where we can immerse ourselves in the experiences and qualities of the house and sign in which it is found. As with any unfamiliar venture in life, we may unintentionally resist or fall back into familiar patterns for security. The old ways of being are symbolized by the house and sign placement of the south node.

The South Node: Past Influences

Known as the Dragon's Tail, the south node represents past, prior life experiences of souls. Its symbol in the birth chart is an upright horseshoe or "u." It indicates areas of life, qualities, and experiences that need to be released or employed in the journey of evolution. As stated earlier, this does not mean we are required to lose the prior lessons, but rather engage the positive aspects of them while pursuing the new lessons of the north node. We use these past lessons to grow, and in service to others.

By utilizing the positive qualities of the south node, we can offer contributions for the greater good of humanity, animals, and the earth. These lessons are ones that we've experienced in prior incarnations, both positive and negative. Because the nodes function as an axis, the energy between them needs to flow in an unrestricted manner. Problems arise when we remain stuck in the south node's (past) influences and resist the north node's urge for new conditions. This can be overcome by using the accumulated wisdom from the past to contribute in new, positive ways through the north node.

The south node is associated with karma in that it shows what we've created in prior incarnations. Although no experience is really bad (except in our thinking of it as so), the north node compels us to move beyond the old and, in so doing, take responsibility for past karmic traits by either balancing them in a more positive, productive way, or by releasing them altogether.

Here's a simple example: Lindsay's south node is in the second house in the sign of Taurus. The second house is concerned with material possessions, property, money, work, non-tangible values, and security. Taurus is associated with the very same issues, as it is the natural sign of the second house in the zodiac. (The natural sign indicates the natural order of the zodiac, beginning with Aries as the first sign and corresponding to the first house.) In prior incarnations and past events, Lindsay's soul may have been overly attached to material possessions, money, and security from her position in life or through partnerships. She may have owned land or a business. She may have been selfish and unwilling to share her resources with others. Ultimately, she would have learned that although these resources are valuable, they are not the enduring treasures of the soul because they are temporary possessions. She is now compelled by her soul's desire to reevaluate her relationship with resources and money as well as her non-tangible values.

On the other end of the axis is the north node in the eighth house in the sign of Scorpio. Since the eighth house is naturally associated with the sign of Scorpio, there is a double emphasis on developing the qualities of this sign: transformation, shared resources, psychology, and the metaphysical. To move in the direction of her north node, Lindsay needs to find value and security in nonmaterial resources such as spirituality, sharing with others, inner strength, and meaningful introspection. She will need to go fearlessly within herself to learn about her psychological makeup, her shadow side, and the true resource of power residing within her own soul. There will be lessons involving shared resources through inheritance and marriage, selflessness, psychological self-assessment, an interest in metaphysics, and inner exploration (Scorpio).

She may find herself appointed as an administrator of family resources as the executor of family wills (also associated with the 8th house). She can apply the old lessons of her south node in meeting the needs of the north node by using them wisely, fairly, and discerningly. She must gravitate away from self-centeredness and selfishness into generosity. Given her natural business acumen of the south node, she can offer guidance and wisdom about resources that benefit others. If she examines her own psychological makeup, she may help others in their psychological examinations (also a non-tangible resource).

How do we recognize when we're moving in the direction of the north node for growth and not falling back into the south? The new lessons of the north node will arise relatively effortlessly, although these new faculties require development and a time investment on our part. We may notice that our pathway is accelerated, and doors to new, exciting experiences open easily. We encounter little resistance on our pathway and meet people who help us assimilate the new lessons. We find ourselves drawn to the energy that the north node beckons us to embrace, study, and express. Events that are supportive of the new lessons appear as if by magic. It feels as though the world is on our side. Our destiny seems to have a will of its own, without our conscious involvement or will. The universe supports us in all ways. We're enthusiastic and passionate about life, and excited about our unfolding potential.

If we're overly attached to the qualities of our south node, we will encounter the opposite. Often, people are tempted to fall into the outworn patterns of the past simply because they are familiar and comfortable. Given that one of the top fears of humans is change, it's easy to see how and why this occurs.

When it does, unhappiness typically ensues. Setbacks and dire circumstances may happen, seemingly for no reason. Things may seem under control and relatively fine, but then an unforeseen event arises to shatter those conditions. I believe this is the case when people complain about being unfulfilled with life, burned out, continually dissatisfied, or depressed. Through these uncomfortable conditions, universal intelligence gives us the message to turn our life around and go in a forward direction. We've become trapped in our own past and need to change.

During difficult times, ponder the direction in which you're heading. Is it a reenactment of old, stale patterns? Do you feel blocked for unknown reasons, despite your best efforts? Chances are you need to reassess the trajectory you're focused on and make adjustments, let go of the past, and fearlessly embrace the new lessons that your soul intended before birth.

Learning About Your Past and Current Soul Lessons

Using one of the many Internet astrology websites, calculate your natal chart. Locate the north node in your chart (symbolized by the upside-down horseshoe). What qualities are associated with its sign and house? These are what your soul needs to learn about, embrace, and express.

Then, look to the south node's placement, directly across from the north. The sign and house of this node are qualities you need to use in fulfillment of the north node's lessons or those you may need to release. Write down several ways that you can use the accumulated wisdom your soul gathered in the past, based on the sign and house placement of the south node. Or, note the undesirable (shadow) qualities of the sign and consider releasing them if you find yourself expressing them.

Remember, the south node represents what we've outgrown, what we need to release, and the wisdom we can use to move forward in our new lessons.

8

Soul Pods and the Wheel of Archetypes

When two souls are one, they hear each other, even in silence.
~ *Matshona Dhliwayo*

It's the spring of 1966 and recess time at my elementary school. I'm playing kickball with classmates in the schoolyard — the only game in which I feel a smidgen of confidence about my athletic abilities. A shy, introverted, sensitive child of eight years old, I feel much more comfortable bonding with animals than people. I struggle to make friends and feel secure, due to my feelings of alienation. I have no idea where I fit in and why I feel lonely most days. I'm nervous and on edge most of the time.

My attention drifts momentarily from the game to the freeway bridge in the near distance. As the cars and trucks whizz by, I think about how lucky the people in them are to be free from the forced rules, regulations, and structures of school. I strain to catch a glimpse of a driver and imagine what that person's life is like. *Where are they going? Probably someplace fun, like shopping, vacationing, or visiting relatives. Gosh, I hate school! I wish I were on that bridge traveling somewhere instead of being trapped in this place.* These thoughts trigger others: *I don't fit in, no matter how hard I try. I make friends and then they talk about me behind my back. I hate my life! Why am I here anyway? I have no one to talk to about how I feel.*

My attention is jolted back to the game field by loud screams of delight for a scored home run. My team is ahead by five points. *It's almost time to go home, where I'll be free to dream, listen to music, play, and do what I want. God, please help me to understand*

what my life is about and why I feel so different from the other kids.
Where are the friends who understand me? What is wrong with me?
I feel like one of those aliens I've read about. The outside bell rings, signaling the end of recess. I run to catch my bus home. I sigh in relief.

I cannot remember a time in my earlier life when I did not wish to be someone other than myself or somewhere other than where I was. As a child, I indulged in the luxury of escapism by fantasizing about living a different life, one in which I enjoyed multiple friendships, had charmingly good looks, was popular among my peers, and felt special in some way. During high school, I pondered which clique I might belong in: the "jocks" (I was not interested in playing sports); the "nerds" (I was on the honor roll but didn't identify with most of the straight A students); the popular kids (the ones who wore the latest fashions, drove their own cars, and hung out with the "in" crowd who never gave me the time of day); or the "heads" (the kids who partied, drank, smoked pot, and got into trouble). I didn't drink at that age but regarded the "heads" as very cool rebels. Of course, there were classmates who didn't fit into any of these groups. I befriended some of them yet still didn't feel connected. Something was missing, and I desperately wanted to discover what that something was.

In my senior year of high school and my early 20s, drugs and alcohol soothed the burning wound of feeling different from others. But soon that "solution" failed and the wound throbbed even more intensely. During my mid-20s, I attended numerous 12-step meetings and successfully recovered, yet I continued to escape through the addiction of diversion and wishful thinking until I began intensive spiritual introspection in my late 30s.

The desire to transcend mundane life gradually lessened in intensity through the internal awareness of self-reflection, honest introspection, and spiritual practices, yet it remains today, although much tempered. The deeply rooted thirst to be someone other than who I am occasionally emerges during times of stress, difficulties, and uncertainty. Remnants of my prior escapism still exist within me. The difference now is that I know the signs, the symptoms, and how to quell them, since I've discovered I am exactly where I need to be at any given time. I will not and cannot be anyone other than myself. The truth I've uncovered is simple, yet profound: I am making passage on the thoroughfare intended by my soul, moment by moment, day by day.

Perhaps you, too, have felt lost, uncertain, alone, discouraged, or fearful about your life's direction. Maybe you've endured a painful childhood, emotional trauma, or a psychological breakdown. You may have suffered the loss of a loved one, fought your way through a serious illness, or experienced the dissolution of a rewarding career. In any case, there *is* a way out, a point of safety, and quiet sanctuary, and it is by following the guidance of your soul.

In this chapter, you will discover how to identify your soul's themes and recognize your kindred soul pod. I explain universal archetypes and how these are expressed in various ways. This chapter delves even deeper into who we are at our core and where we are going in life, based on our soul's intent. In the midst of difficult times and life transitions, I believe we need to be reminded, renewed, and motivated by the soul's aspirations because these are the enduring qualities that we will take with us when we return to our spiritual home someday. When life gets troublesome and confusing, it's helpful to focus on the spiritual lessons and values we've set out to master. The more self-knowledge we have, the better we live. The following client story illustrates the initial stage of awakening to the promptings of the soul.

Messages from Kristin's Soul

"I need your insight about where I fit in," Kristin explains at the start of a session. "I just turned 40 and I should know this, but

I don't. What I mean is, I think maybe I've missed my calling. I've worked at different jobs, am married, and have a daughter, but I've been waking up at night with anxiety about my life. I feel kind of stupid asking this, but is this all there is to life? I'm getting older and I want to feel something more than what I do now. I want to make a difference in the world. Does this even make sense?"

Before I can respond, Kristin blurts out another concern. "The other thing that bothers me is not having friends. I've tried to fit in with groups of people from my work and neighborhood, but I don't feel connected to them. They talk about sports or TV shows — things I'm not interested in. I don't have anything to say to them."

I pause and tune into Kristin's soul before responding. A strong, unmistakable intuitive impression comes: I sense that she's in a quandary about "fitting in" because she hasn't fully grasped her soul's specific vibration — what qualities, natural inclinations, and skills she radiates. So, she drifts here and there, hoping to feel fulfilled, yet never actually experiences acceptance or connection. In the past, she tried to mold herself to fit in with others, but didn't resonate with them. *How can I best relay this to help her?* I ponder. As usual, I turn to those in spirit for help. My spirit team is ready and willing to facilitate the session by impressing me with guidance to impart.

"It would be helpful to take some time to really get to know yourself," I begin. "Think about all of the things that make your life worthwhile — specifically, the qualities and activities that *do* fulfill you. What makes your heart sing and brings you joy? What do you feel passionate about? These things are not necessarily your paid work. Can you name a few of those now?"

"Um, well, I never really thought about that. Let me see."

I wait patiently as she considers this for a few moments.

"I like to help kids in any way I can," Kristin says softly. "I have a big heart for those who didn't have a good home. I volunteered at a homeless shelter several years ago, watching the kids while their moms went to see about getting jobs and other business. But that's all I did. I didn't consider it a big deal. Is this what you mean?"

"That's exactly what Spirit is asking you to think about! You see, you belong to a group of souls who share a similar expression of the higher consciousness of God, those who love to help children. This means you are drawn to care for them in various ways. No way is right or wrong; they are all expressions of your specific soul pod. In fact, my spirit team shows that you've done this very service in prior incarnations, even though you don't remember it. This is why you are drawn to it: you have done it before and this life is an extension of that. There are new things to learn with this theme."

I sense Kristin is startled by this information. "But is that my life purpose?" she asks. "Should I get some type of education, a degree maybe, to do this work?"

"Not necessarily. Anytime we express a divine quality such as nurturing, that expression is part of our life purpose because we are Spirit, first and foremost, in a physical form. Purpose doesn't always refer to what we do for a living; it is how we express our soul's divine qualities. There are many different soul pods in the world. Each has a specific mission to carry out in life. We often travel through lifetimes with our soul pod because we resonate energetically with them. We are naturally drawn to them and they to us. They can be friends, family, work associates, neighbors, or people who volunteer alongside of us. The common bond or quality they share is the 'ray' of God they are expressing. *Ray* means the radiation of God coming from your soul. In your case, that ray is helping children. When we express our ray and meet fellow pod members who are doing the same, we immediately feel comfortable with them. Our service is multiplied by working with others."

"Oh, this is good to know!" Kristin exclaims. "Should I go back to volunteering? I left because I became overwhelmed by the children's pain and fear. It was hard for me to bear." Her voice cracks. "These innocent children were hurt." Clearly, her experiences touched her deeply.

"Maybe. My spirit team advises that doing this type of work is one of the things you came into life to do. You must release the prior-life experiences of witnessing so much pain and suffering with children to carry on these lessons. You see, your soul evolves by helping others. Often, the trying circumstances in life are precisely the ones we ourselves need to grow. The team says that you met other shelter volunteers whom you liked. They are from your same soul pod. Your presence at the shelters made a difference, perhaps more than you realize."

"Yes, I met two women at the shelter who I often chatted with," Kirstin confirms. "I sensed they wanted to help the kids as much as I did."

The end of the session arrives and Kristin thanks me profusely for the insight. "I'm going to see about signing up at the shelters again," she says in parting.

Soul Pods

Over many years of sessions and metaphysical studies, I've discovered that each of us belongs to a specific *soul pod*, a group of souls who express the same or similar qualities. Many people belong to more than one, although one generally appears to be dominant.

The themes expressed by a soul pod are particular *archetypes* — or, deeply engrained patterns of behavior, thoughts or symbols imprinted in our unconscious mind. The concept of archetypes in human collective consciousness was put forth by Swiss psychoanalyst Carl Jung in 1919. Jung believed that these patterns of thought forms were universal, inherited, and naturally found in the human unconscious. Examples of archetypes are "Mother," "Father," "Hero," "Teacher," and "Caregiver." The soul pod expresses these traits throughout life and in service to others. They are often karmic in nature because souls have developed or worked with them in previous incarnations. I will discuss the qualities of some common archetypes later in this chapter.

We're naturally drawn to others in our soul pod due to the law of attraction. Have you ever met someone and instantly felt at home in their presence? Chances are that person is from your soul pod. You may have noticed that the conversation you engaged in flowed easily and perhaps conveyed a nonverbal, intuitive understanding. The person may have been a stranger to you, but you felt an unmistakable bond, the exchange of a similar consciousness and comfort. Several minutes into the conversation, you may have found yourself nodding in agreement with what the person was expressing. There was an easy rapport between the two of you from the start. Sharing a soul pod does not necessarily mean that souls have been together in prior lifetimes, although this is a possibility. The mutual resonance comes from a shared spiritual consciousness, and intuitive, empathic understanding.

Soul pods are comprised of individuals who are either in spirit or in the physical world. Those in spirit may be part of our spirit team, helping us in our earthly lives. Or they may be souls we've known in prior incarnations who happen to be in spirit at the time when we are on the physical plane. In planning our incarnation, we may have consulted with them in the spirit world and agreed to work together. These souls contribute to our earthly lives through inspiration. To continue with the example of Kristin, her spirit team inspired her to engage with displaced children — playing with them, talking with them, reading stories to them, and reassuring them. Our soul pod does not control us; rather, they give us intuitive nudges when necessary.

Throughout numerous sessions, I've witnessed soul pod members in the spirit world carry out their agreements with clients. Staying with the example of caring for children, I've read for people who've worked in child protective services, and also those who do psychological counseling for children who have suffered sexual abuse. One memorable session was with a woman who was a child psychologist and counseled individuals at an inner-city resource center. During the session, I was aware of a soul in spirit who appeared as a young boy with a playful, lighthearted personality, about five years old. I silently asked him what his mission was with the client.

He responded, "I help her with her work with children. I inspire her about what will help the children she works with — how to get through to them, how to make them laugh and rise above the sadness of their lives. I help her to create games that lift the spirits of these children."

In another session, a client who writes novels was accompanied by a peculiar, eccentric-looking man in spirit (he appeared in a brightly flowered suit, a spiked haircut and red-framed glasses). He impressed me that he belonged to the soul pod expressing the archetype of the "artist." When I relayed this to the client, she said, "I think I've seen him in my dreams! When I write my novels, I ask the muses for inspiration. On one occasion, I got a glimpse of him in my mind's eye. He is wild looking and somewhat eccentric! That's astonishing that he's here in this session! I've always felt that someone was collaborating with me when I write."

Expressions of Various Archetypes

To help you determine which soul pod and archetype your soul connects with, I've compiled a list of some of the most common groups I've observed in my work, along with their characteristics. You'll also find the shadow expression (the incorrect use of the qualities) of each.

Please note that it's possible to have connection with more than one group. As you read the descriptions, notice how you feel about them. Which do you resonate with and readily recognize? Particularly note how you may already be expressing the qualities of that group in your life. Which one feels right, based on your life experiences and soul's calling?

- **The Caregiver:** Nurturing, selfless giver, compassionate, interested in others' well-being. Shadow: martyrdom, needs to be needed, self-sacrificing.
- **The Healer:** Similar to the Caregiver. Embraces spiritual consciousness, ethical, intuitive, sees the connection among all, humble. Shadow: arrogant, unethical, deceptive.
- **The System Buster:** Passionate about change, visionary, transformative, challenger of the status quo. Shadow: rebellion for its own sake, disagreeable, stubborn, instigator of chaos.
- **The Creator:** Imaginative, free-thinking, nonlinear thinker, visionary. Shadow: disorganized, scattered, impractical.
- **The Peacemaker/Negotiator:** Fair and open-minded, justice-seeking, impartial, cooperative, nonjudgmental. Shadow: controlling, argumentative, manipulative, hard-nosed in perspectives.
- **The Teacher:** Wise, sincere in helping others to learn, communicative of knowledge, action-taking (in applying knowledge to life), humble. Shadow: selfish with knowledge, overly rational, manipulative, authoritarian, action-less in applying knowledge to life.
- **The Policy Makers:** Group oriented, sincerity in improving existing systems, goal-oriented, humanitarian, selfless service to society. Shadow: self-seeking, materially-focused, controlling, narcissistic, arrogant.

- **The Scientist:** Desires discovery to help humanity, animals, and the earth; open-minded, curious, probing, intelligent, humanitarian. Shadow: uses knowledge and discoveries to control others, prejudiced concerning data, overly intellectual, condescending.
- **The Innovator:** Similar to the Scientist. Clever-minded, intuitive, problem solver, inventive, futuristic, improvement-minded. Shadow: rebellious, notoriety-seeking, arrogant, one-dimensional thinker.
- **The Spiritual Leader:** Peace-seeking, spiritually-centered, teaches and practices natural laws, radiates compassion and authentic spiritual wisdom, fair-minded, selfless, healing. Shadow: ignores own flaws, doesn't live the principles espoused, exploits the vulnerable through manipulation, materially-oriented.
- **The Traveler:** Gathers knowledge and experience through visiting or studying various cultures, shares knowledge gained through adventure and exploration, sees unity among all cultures. Shadow: escapes life by constantly being on the move, wanders without purpose, ungrounded.
- **The Way-Shower:** Models ideas, behavior and innovation to help others, implements new ways of being, works to dissolve outworn patterns in families, groups and society. Shadow: manipulative, self-seeking, seeks change without legitimate cause, chaos-loving.
- **The Warrior:** Courageous, bold, fearless, assertive, heroic. Shadow: foolish, unwise risk-taking, falsely proud, violent.

As you can see, several of the soul pod archetypes overlap with similar qualities expressed among them. Rather than assigning hard boundaries between groups, we can view them as intertwining with shared attributes. Identifying with an archetype is not meant to define or limit your entire identity to that set of qualities, but to help you recognize your soul's ray or calling. You may express a few of the listed qualities or additional ones not listed. The archetypes are a useful guide when considering where you fit in, what your strengths and skills are, as well as how you might convey them in the external world. They are useful for people who seek guidance on specific fields, occupations, and services they feel drawn to.

The shadow side of the archetypes arise when the listed qualities are used unwisely, selfishly, without moderation, or to excess. For example, someone who expresses qualities of the Caregiver can fall prey to the self-centered demand to be needed. He may base his self-worth and his own ego-centered desires on rescuing those he perceives as weak or vulnerable. From this, he obtains power and his sense of self. This is not the healthy use of the archetype ... far from it.

I've also witnessed people, especially women, who become exhausted and ill from too much caregiving, without regard for their own self-care. In many cases, if and when they do engage in self-care, they feel guilty. At times, these people have no recognition of what they are doing — blindly following the dictates of family expectations, rigid gender roles, or assuming a martyrdom complex.

In another instance, a soul who is from the pod that expresses the archetype of the Spiritual Leader may use her power arrogantly, for material gain or the exploitation of unsuspecting people. As stated earlier, there have been so-called spiritual leaders who have engaged in these behaviors, much to the detriment of others and themselves. The fall from the false pedestal of grandeur is great and karma must be met in these cases.

As with all things in life, balance is the key to successful living, happiness, and service to others. If you feel lethargic, discouraged, or directionless — no matter the particular archetype — honest self-examination is crucial to regaining balance. By doing this regularly, you will be able to correct extremes that throw you off course.

The Soul's Journey as Depicted in the Archetypes of the Tarot

Years ago, I purchased a deck of Rider-Waite Tarot cards out of curiosity. I knew about the 78-card deck from acquaintances who used them for psychic insights, but had never explored the spiritual symbolism and esoteric meanings of the cards. I was excited to discover what information I could obtain through using them so bought several books to help guide me in learning. At the time, I didn't realize just how valuable the cards would become for my own personal intuitive development and for clients during life guidance sessions. I use them as insightful tools to access the past, present, and likely future of specific situations. Also of value is the assessment of specific energies that are at play in the situation, based on the cards that are drawn.

The deck consists of 22 major arcana cards (archetypes), 40 minor arcana cards (mundane, everyday circumstances), and 16 court (people) cards. There are four suits in the deck, each associated with one of the universal elements of fire, air, water, and earth. Each of the 22 major arcana cards describes archetypes and themes of the soul in its journey from birth throughout life. Because the archetypes indicate specific ingrained, universal thought patterns, all souls will experience and express each archetype at one time or another throughout multiple lifetimes in varying degrees. Each card uses unique symbolism with images and colors congruent with their archetypal meaning.

In my zest to learn the meanings of the cards, I decided to pull several cards daily to interpret and study them. How would they apply to my life? What would they reveal? I was eager to find out. The daunting task of learning the meanings of all 78 cards seemed more digestible when broken down into small, daily increments. So, I began by pulling three cards from the deck and using the books as a guide.

In the beginning, I applied only the mundane meanings (the minor arcana) of the cards to my life. Sometime later, I desired to plunge more deeply into the major arcana cards, particularly as they relate to the spiritual journey of souls. The most significant development occurred when I was able to immediately gain an intuitive impression upon viewing a card. Surprisingly, the cards appeared to take on a life of their own beyond my rational understanding of what I'd read about them. They spoke to me. The more I used the cards, the stronger these impressions became. They resonated with the archetypes of my own unconscious. Eventually they became a portal through which I could perceive not only the future, but the dynamics of a current situation or event. After months of self-use, I mustered enough confidence to incorporate them into my client readings. I also eventually developed workshops to help others use the cards for guidance in their spiritual journeys.

On a side note, the artist of the Rider-Waite deck is Pamela Colman Smith, who illustrated many books from the late 1800s through the early 1900s. The Rider-Waite deck is the most widely used deck of the tarot and much tribute is due to Smith; her engaging images and artistry have made it popular. In my opinion, she captured the essence of each archetype beautifully in the scenes, symbolism, and colors of each card.

For our purposes here, we will focus on the major arcana only — specifically on how they depict the spiritual evolution and journey of the soul from birth to death. I've listed the descriptions of each image on the cards and their associated major themes/archetypes.

If you own the Rider-Waite deck, it's helpful to view each card as you read its meaning below. The images will appear to "pop out" to you, and I suggest viewing each through the lens of intuition. If you'd like to purchase the deck, it's available for sale online through various retail sellers.

As you read the significance of each major arcana below, determine which you identify with, those you deeply embrace, and those that feel unfamiliar. Notice which descriptions stand out, those that speak to you at this time in your life, and the ones that you feel drawn to investigate more deeply.

0. **The Fool:** The image of a young, carefree man, holding a hobo stick and pouch, standing at the edge of a mountaintop, with a small, white dog by his feet and the sun behind him. The background of this card is yellow. Archetype: *The Child*. The soul in its purity at birth, ready to set out on the journey of physical life. As arcana 0, the fool symbolizes pure potentiality, lack of experience, purity, innocence, and risk-taking. The color yellow is indicative of optimism and hopefulness, as the sun shown above.

1. **The Magician:** A red-robed man standing with one arm in the air and the other pointing down to the earth. In his upward hand, he holds a wand (indicating a conduit) with the infinity symbol above his head. On a table in front of him are the symbols of each suit of the deck: a sword (thought), a wand (inspiration and creativity), a cup (emotion, relationships, and spirituality), and a pentacle (earth, practical resources, the body). Archetype: *The Creator* who uses all of his/her resources to convert thoughts and desires into reality; the right use of personal will as a co-creator with God. The color red is symbolic of the root energy center of the body connected with the earth.

2. **The High Priestess:** A blue-robed woman with a jeweled crown (moon stone) sitting between two pillars — one black, the other white. A crescent moon is intertwined in

her robe. Archetype: *The Intuitive; spiritual insight and truth.* The crescent moon (an early phase of the moon in its cycle) is symbolic of inner reflection, higher sense perception, and the increase of esoteric, spiritual knowledge. The black-and-white pillars symbolize the combination of the yin (female) and yang (male) within the individual. Both are necessary to combine in the journey of life.

3. **The Empress:** A matronly woman with a crown sits on a throne in nature, holding a scepter. At her right side is the Roman symbol of the Venus mirror, representing femininity, love, friendship, fertility, and motherhood. Archetype: *The Mother and the Divine Feminine.* Represents nurturing, unconditional love, creativity, nature, and abundance.

4. **The Emperor:** An older man with a beard and a crown sits upon a square throne, holding a scepter. Archetype: *The Father and the Divine Masculine.* The emperor wears a red robe (like the Magician of Arcana I), symbolic of the root energy center. This archetype encompasses worldly experience, paternal guidance, strong business acumen, and rational thinking. The Emperor's beard is symbolic of wisdom he's accumulated in the material world and often through business.

5. **The Hierophant:** Often referred to as the "Pope" of the tarot deck, a robed man on a throne sits between pillars with two devotees/servants below. He holds a golden scepter in his hand and wears a crown. His hand is raised in blessing. Archetype: *Traditional religions, established societal order, and doctrines.* The two pillars represent the duality of earthly consciousness: the yin and the yang. The men below the Hierophant represent the hierarchy of organized religion in dutiful service.

6. **The Lovers:** A man and a woman stand naked in the Garden of Eden with Archangel Raphael appearing above

them with arms outstretched in a blessing. A snake winds around a tree filled with fruit. Archetype: *The Divine Masculine and Feminine, duality, good and evil, choice.* This card represents the union of the yin and yang within each soul. Both are necessary to achieve harmony. The serpent is symbolic of the devil in Christian mythology and of self-serving choice. Significantly, this archetype represents the free will given to humans by the Creator.

7. **The Chariot:** A man with a golden crown steers a chariot pulled by a white and a black sphinx. In his hand he holds a wand; on his uniform shoulders are crescent moons. The wings of the Roman messenger god Hermes appear on the front of the chariot. Archetype: *The power of the personal will, ambition, stamina, focus, success, and forward movement.* The charioteer harnesses and blends the forces of both dark and light in his life to move forward. Additionally, this card represents personal responsibility while piloting life.

8. **Strength:** A woman in a white robe adorned with flowers uses her hands to fearlessly open the mouth of a lion. The infinity symbol floats above her head. Archetype: *Rejuvenation from illness or adverse conditions, the force within oneself to overcome difficulties in life, courage, determination, and fearlessness.* The white dress is symbolic of the pure, divine soul while the lion represents the personality, the ego, and earthly desires. The infinity sign indicates the ever-flowing, unlimited, abundant power of the Creator.

9. **The Hermit:** A bearded man in a gray, hooded robe looks downward while holding a staff in one hand and a lantern with a star in the other. Archetype: *Spiritual guidance through study, introspection, prayer, and meditation; going within; a period of isolation.* The star in the hermit's lantern symbolizes the light of the Creator within. His

beard and staff represent wisdom and spiritual guidance, respectively.

10. **The Wheel of Fortune:** A wheel with eight radiating spokes. In the four corners are symbols of the four fixed signs of the zodiac: Taurus (bull), Scorpio (eagle), Leo (lion), and Aquarius (angel). The sphinx resting on top of the wheel represents the wisdom and stability of the universe. This card is related to the Lovers, arcana six, because it indicates the power of our will to change the course of our life. In numerology, the number 10 reduces to a 1 — indicating the beginning of a new cycle in life. Archetype: *The flow of life (symbolized by the wheel's continual movement), the power to make decisions, the natural law of perpetual motion, and the creation of favorable circumstances through free will.* This card also represents karma (the Law of Cause and Effect) and our ability to change our destiny through personal choice.

11. **Justice:** A robed man sits holding a sword in his right hand and balanced scales in his left. Archetype: *Karmic and earthly justice, reaping what we sow, fairness through natural laws.* The sword is symbolic of the cutting away of illusion to reveal the truth. Archangel Michael is often depicted holding the sword of justice. The scales are symbols of the justice and fairness of karmic law.

12. **The Hanged Man:** A man hangs upside down from a tree with his hands folded behind his back. His head emanates a golden aura. Archetype: *Employing elevated perspective to situations, events and circumstances in one's life; a period of adjustment to consider one's options; a pause; a shift from the perspective of the personality and ego to that of the Higher Self.* The golden aura symbolizes the spiritual enlightenment which all humans must evolve towards. This arcana suggests the natural Law of Rhythm (the ebb and flow of life), specifically the time period for introspection versus action.

13. **Death:** A skeleton wearing a black suit of armor holding a flag with a white flower on it rides on a white horse. Beneath him on a battlefield is a dead body as the sun rises over the horizon behind him. Archetype: *Transformation, spiritual release, evolution from old ways of being, shedding of the old to embrace the new.* The white flower on the flag represents the life force that always triumphs over evil and physical death. This card symbolizes perpetual change during life, and the need to discard the old to evolve.

14. **Temperance:** Archangel Michael stands on the bank of a pond with one foot on land and one in the water. He holds a cup in either hand and mixes a liquid between the two. Archetype: *Achievement of balance and moderation in one's life, harmony between unconscious and conscious influences, cooperation with others, adaptation, and flexibility.* The sun rising from behind symbolizes success from careful moderation and blending.

15. **The Devil:** A beastly figure with goat horns and wings sits above a man and woman who are chained together. On his right palm is the astrological symbol for Saturn, planet of limitation and earthly consciousness; in his left is a torch. Archetype: *Destruction arising from unbalanced materialism, evil, addictions to earthly/carnal pleasures, temptation.* The man and woman chained together represent unhealthy or destructive relationships.

16. **The Tower:** A tall tower is struck by lightning, causing flames to erupt from its windows. A man and woman fall from the tower. Note that this card follows that of the Devil, the wrong use of one's will. Destruction and chaos are the result. Archetype: *Change, destruction of the old structures of one's life, annihilation of materially-centered living.* The golden crown to the right of the tower symbolizes divine will.

17. **The Star:** A kneeling woman pours water from a vessel into a pool. One foot is in the water as she kneels on the bank. Above her is a large, golden star, surrounded by seven smaller ones. Archetype: *Cosmic assistance, the Divine, prayers answered, communion with the Creator through meditation, and higher awareness.* It's significant that this card follows the destruction symbolized by the Tower, assuring hope and healing after chaos, destruction, illness, or loss.

18. **The Moon:** A wolf and a dog look up at the moon beside a river from which a crayfish crawls forth. Archetype: *The unconscious realm, all that is hidden, dreams, intuition, deception.* This card symbolizes the inherent unconscious forces within each of us, and intuitive messages from the subconscious.

19. **The Sun:** A naked child rides a white horse, holding an unfurled red banner. The sun blazes above him and sunflowers appear behind him. Archetype: *Success, freedom, attainment, happiness, children, simplicity.* The child symbolizes innocence and enjoyment of the simple pleasures of life. The sun is symbolic of the successful attainment of goals.

20. **Judgement:** Archangel Gabriel blows a golden trumpet, adorned with an emblem of the redemptive cross. Beneath are men, women and children, seemingly arising from death and coffins. Archetype: *A spiritual awakening, regeneration, renewal, completion of a cycle, lifting of consciousness from the material to the spiritual, rebirth.*

21. **The World:** A woman, clothed only in a banner, holds a wand in either hand. She is surrounded by a wreath. In each corner is the image of an animal representing the four elements: fire, air, earth, and water. Archetype: *The completion of a cycle of evolution, success, attainment, spiritual consciousness integration, liberation, the completion*

of an earthly life. Note that this final arcana is represented by a circle (the wreath) as is the first arcana, the Fool. This symbolizes the completion of one cycle of spiritual development and the initiation of a new one.

As you can see, the tarot is a pictorial representation of various archetypes contained within the human experience from birth to death. The cards give insight, direction, and clarity in our unfolding spiritual evolution. Here is a simple exercise you can use for your personal journey.

Your Personal Tarot Drawing

From the 78 cards of the tarot deck, remove the 22 major arcana cards and place them in front of you. (For ease in recognition, they are the cards with words printed beneath the images.) Keep a pen and paper handy to write your impressions.

Pull one card of the 22 and write your impressions of the images on it. What stands out to you? What colors are prominent? How does its meaning apply to your life in the present?

If you do this exercise daily, note how the archetype of the card reveals itself to you throughout the day. You can also choose one card and do a brief meditation on it. What does your intuition reveal?

9

The Gateway to Eternity: Practices for Higher Consciousness and Healing

What you are is God's gift to you, what you become is your gift to God.
~ Hans Urs von Balthasar

At this point, you may be wondering how to get "there" from "here," especially if you are currently in the midst of working through wakeup calls, challenges, and blocks that seem to be holding up your progress. Particularly in these uncertain times in which we all live, you may wish to know how to maintain hope, gratitude, forgiveness, and optimism in your daily life. For this reason, the focus of this chapter is on practical things that you can do, in the form of exercises and meditations that will help you reach these higher states of consciousness during both good and bad times.

There is no magic wand that can instantly make us feel better. There's no one "answer" that, if found, will erase all of our troubles or explain why they happened in the first place. But the choice to rise above difficulties always exists. Do your best to acknowledge your pain, confusion, and exasperation, then intend to focus *above* and *beyond* them. Know that you are not defeated by anything in life, except by your own permission to be so.

This plan of action is the only way forward. Through acknowledgment comes acceptance and the end of resistance to the way life currently is. It may be too soon to see how and why life is as it is; the time may not yet be ripe for that level of discernment, if it comes at all. Since the only available time that truly exists is now, that is what you must seize: the present moment. This is where all healing arises — not in the past or future. *Right here*, in this very moment, is the power you possess.

In this final chapter, we'll explore how to shift your focus from whatever is troubling you to the more elevated perspective of your soul's consciousness. To be clear, this does not mean to ignore, suppress, or deny what is happening. Instead, you will recognize the presence of your feelings, accept them, and refocus on the part of you that lies beyond them. By doing so, you will avoid allowing hardships to define you, and instead recognize their role in strengthening you.

When first practicing these exercises, you may find that you can do them for only a short time — a few moments, perhaps. There is no harm in that whatsoever. A few minutes a day is sufficient to build your awareness. I recommend doing one exercise in the morning to start your day, and one in the evening to conclude it. As time goes on, you may want to add an exercise midday or lengthen the time you spend on each. There's no right way. Your practice will be as unique as you. The important point is to make time to do them consistently.

As a reminder, one of the most common issues people have while doing contemplative exercises is the inability to stop their thoughts. I've heard students mention this time after time when teaching intuitive and mediumistic development workshops. This mind noise is normal and expected. The mind's job is to produce thoughts, after all!

So, it's best to bring it along in your journey, much as you would a beloved companion. Don't fight against it, wrestle with it, or resist it. View your mind as a friend, not an adversary. When thoughts of yesterday or tomorrow come up during exercises, simply notice them and refocus on your breath or body awareness. Most of all, do not think you have failed in the exercise. You will discover that the longer you practice stillness, the less you will contend with intrusive thoughts. There is no goal to the exercises; there is only the experience of who you are, beyond your thoughts.

As you begin to practice the exercises, keep a pen and paper nearby. Make notes about how you feel doing the practice, what thoughts drift in, and how you feel afterwards. Importantly, check in with the condition of your body and mind. For example, write a few words about your level of stress, any tension in your body, and any locations in the body that feel tense or out of balance. You will not have to do this as you progress. This is helpful when assessing how valuable a particular exercise is to you. Some may be more effective than others, depending on your unique needs.

Engage Present Time Awareness

Most people find it difficult to engage present-time awareness in the busyness of everyday life. Hectic schedules, multiple diversions, taking on too much, and being surrounded by continual noise and chaos create stress, confusion, and internal pressure. This can lead to problems, such as feeling overwhelmed, mental overload, and various physical symptoms. These simple exercises are designed to retrain your focus to be in the moment.

1. **Basic Breath Exercise:** I call this exercise "home base" because it is the foundation you can return to, time after time. The breath is always available in every moment and functions as the vehicle to transport your consciousness to the place of stillness within. Remember, the point is not to cease all thinking but to go beyond it to the inner sanctuary of peace.

   Before beginning, remove all distractions from your environment. Turn off phones, TVs, and the Internet. On a piece of paper, write a few words that describe how you feel and what thoughts you currently have. Do not judge; just observe these and write them down.

Sit in a comfortable chair (you do not want it to be so comfortable that you fall asleep). Close your eyes. Begin by placing all of your attention on your breath. Follow your breath as it comes in and exits. If thoughts drift in, simply notice them and refocus on your breath. Repeat this for a few minutes. Open your eyes and notice how you feel. How is your stress level? Your emotions? Write a few words about your experience.

2. **Body Awareness:** Begin as you did in the first exercise. After focusing on your breath for a few moments, shift your attention to your body, beginning with the feet. Slowly move up the body to the head, placing your attention on each part of the body. Each time you shift your attention, imagine you are withdrawing your focus from one part of the body and placing it on the next. When you are complete (at the head), return your focus to the rise and fall of your chest. Open your eyes and write a few words about your observations.

3. **Expanded Body Awareness:** This exercise is identical to the previous one, except when focusing on each body part, linger at each and go deeper in awareness to observe any sensations that may appear. If there are none, that's fine. If there are, make note of them and then withdraw your attention to move onto the next part of the body.

   After reaching the head, shift your attention to encompass your entire body, from toes to head. Imagine your life force expanding outward until it fills the entire room. Then expand further to the landscape outdoors, the neighborhood, and beyond to the world. To finish, bring your attention back to the breath, to the rise and fall of your chest. Open your eyes and make note of how you feel.

4. **Being in the Moment with Tasks:** Choose an everyday task that you would normally perform hastily, such as

brushing your teeth, eating, doing dishes, running the vacuum, bathing, showering, or getting dressed. As you begin the task, keep your attention on each movement you make in performing it. Instead of rushing through it, be intentional about noting each sensation and movement. If bathing, for example, feel the water on your skin and notice the sensations that arise as it washes over you. As you wash, be in each movement during the process. Feel the life force in your muscles as they move.

When thoughts arise, allow them to drift away and refocus on your movements. Feel the aliveness in your hands as they perform these actions. As you dry off, become aware of the sensation of the towel on your skin. When combing your hair, "be" in each stroke of the brush or comb. You can use this exercise with any routine task. Notice any sensations that come up during the exercise. Write a few sentences about your experiences.

5. **Present-Time Awareness During Conversations:** This exercise will help you to become a better, more tuned-in listener. You can practice it either in person or on the phone. (It's easier to do it while on the phone because there are less distractions such as body movements, appearance, and eye contact.)

During the conversation, place your attention on listening intently to the other person. Note tone of voice, inflections of speech, pauses, and word emphasis. While listening, keep your attention on the other person's communication and not what your response to it might be. Really tune into what this person is expressing. If possible, also note what emotions and thoughts arise in you while listening. When the other person pauses for your response, breathe deeply before responding. What have you discovered? Did you notice subtleties in the communication that had gone unnoticed before?

Meditations to Reduce Mind Noise

Many times, we allow our noisy mind to dominate the comforting solace of our soul's whispers of peace. Although we can't stop the mind from doing what is does best — think — we can subdue the noise by finding the place of stillness within where the soul resides. This core self often remains obscured and voiceless beneath the clamor of the mind. Yet it is crucial to visit this hidden sanctuary as often as possible, especially when difficult times emerge. Instead of allowing the clanging narrative of the mind to lead us, we can instead choose to encompass ourselves in the serenity and soft whispers of the soul.

These meditations will guide you to that place of safety, quiet, and peace that resides within you. You need no special tools to practice these. All that is required is your focus.

1. **The Garden of Serenity:** Remove distractions from your environment. Sit comfortably in a chair with your spine straight, feet on the floor, and relax. Begin by focusing on your breath — the vehicle that will lead you to the sanctuary of your soul. After a few moments of breath focus, imagine a sparkling column of white light appears directly in front of you. Gently merge with this column of light, feeling it lifting you higher and higher. Feel the light encompass you, enfold you in its warmth, and soothe you.

   Touch down in a beautiful summer garden, filled with brightly colored flowers, tall trees, and a bubbling stream. Open your inner senses to experience the serenity and harmony here. Immerse yourself in the peace as you explore the garden. Walk to the stream and kneel beside it. Gaze deeply into the water. What do you see? What images arise?

   Drink in the stillness as you continue to focus on the beauty of the garden.

Feel your entire body relax, cares and worries cease, and peace wash over you. After a few moments, return to the column of white light. Feel it envelop you as you slowly return to waking consciousness. Focus again on your breath. Feel your feet and hands. Open your eyes. Enjoy the refreshment.

2. **Ray of Divine Light:** Become still and begin by focusing on your breath. After a few moments, turn your attention to the base of your spine — the energy center that is your connection to the earth. Become aware of your legs and feet. Next, shift your attention to the top of your head — the crown energy center that connects you to the source of all life.

   Now imagine that a beam of violet light descends from above the building and enters the crown energy center. Feel it travel down your spinal column into the base of your spine and down through both legs into your feet. See it emerge from the bottoms of your feet and circulate upwards like a fountain. It again descends through the top of your head and travels the length of your spinal column. As it does, imagine it dissolving mental stress, discomfort in the body, and emotional imbalances. See these dissolving in the light.

   When the light reaches your feet this time, ground it into the earth. Now focus on your heart. Allow your heart to soften and open. Picture a vortex of emerald green light emanating from your heart, traveling further and further, out into the world. Now come back to focus on your breath. Feel your feet and hands. Open your eyes.

3. **Make Peace with Disturbing Thoughts:** This exercise helps to eliminate fearful, troubling thoughts by accepting them. Although this appears to be counterintuitive on the surface, acceptance and surrender (instead of denial and

suppression) reduce resistance to these types of thoughts. They are given space to be exactly as they are when we acknowledge their presence but do not attach to them or empower them as the ultimate "truth." Ordinarily, we want to rid ourselves of these types of thoughts as soon as they arise; but what happens if instead of attacking them, we embrace them?

This process helps to reduce our refusal of them (which strengthens them), allowing them to be exactly as they are. By exposing ourselves to the discomfort, we lessen their intensity, much like confronting phobias. Use this meditation when repetitive or disturbing thoughts steal your inner peace.

Begin by noting where in your body the troublesome thoughts appear to be lodged. Is your stomach churning or your heart racing? Is your breath fast and shallow? Perhaps your body feels tense in specific areas — your shoulders, spine, or legs. Focus on this body part filled with tension. As you do, allow the disturbing thought(s) to arise in your consciousness. Observe the thought without judging it. Allow it to replay several times. Now consciously place relaxation into the tense body areas by first feeling the tension and then using your breath to infuse them with relaxation. Feel the tenseness and then the relaxation alternate.

Repeat this alternation throughout the entire body. If the thoughts continue to arise, surrender to them again by acknowledging their presence. This "exposure" to troubling thoughts meditation may take several attempts for noticeable differences.

4. **Become the Observer:** This exercise is similar to the one above, but makes use of different imagery. Use this when you need to detach from worrisome, anxious, or troubling thoughts.

Begin by focusing on your breath for a few moments. Next, imagine you are on a mountaintop, high above a landscape, gazing below. Allow the scene to unfold on your internal viewing screen. Become the observer of all you see from your elevated vantage point. Perhaps you see activity taking place in your vision: vehicles traveling on a road, people milling about, lights flickering in buildings below, or clouds slowly moving over the scene from above. At first, simply observe what images appear.

When you feel complete in this observation, imagine that each of the images represents one of your troubling thoughts. From your vantage point on the mountain, you see the thoughts apart from yourself. You are the witness of the thoughts, but are not attached to them. You are the observer. They function apart from you as hollow images. Stay on this observation platform for a few moments. Return to your breath, feel your legs and feet. Open your eyes.

Exercises to Lessen Painful Emotions

At various times, we feel grief, sadness, loneliness, anger, regret, or disappointment. Emotions are temporary expressions stemming from the thoughts our mind produces. They become troublesome when they linger for long periods. This can take place for a number of reasons, depending on our personal psychological ability to cope, the state of our physical health, fear of change, or our own resistance to giving them up (for one reason or another).

In the case of the latter, I've encountered people who are resistant to giving up grief over the loss of a loved one because they believe this means they are being disloyal to that loved one. An example of this is the thought, *If I don't continually grieve my mother, it means I didn't really love her.* Of course, as I mentioned in an earlier chapter, this is not true; the length of time spent grieving does not equal how much we loved someone. If you have recurring or frequent painful emotions, step back from them using these exercises.

1. **Visualize the Emotion:** When the emotion arises, find a quiet space and close your eyes. Have a sheet of paper or journal and pen nearby. Breathe deeply and "call forth" the emotion to appear in a form on your internal viewing screen. This can appear in any form; allow the image to shape itself as it will without judgment. There is no correct image. Notice the specifics of the image — its size, color, shape. These are clues to how you perceive the emotion and the placement of it in your consciousness.

    Next, imagine the image speaks to you intuitively. What message does it communicate? How does the message feel? What emotions arise? Do not fall into the trap of believing you are "making it up."

    Now ask the image to change form in your mind's eye. What new form does this transformation take? Note the differences between the original image and this new one. Ask this new image to impart a message to you. When you feel complete, open your eyes and write your impressions. What have you discovered?

2. **Bond with the Emotion:** This exercise is done in the same manner as the first but includes a twist. When the image of the troubling emotion forms, imagine it offers you a valuable insight which also appears as an image. This insight is aligned with the elevated wisdom of your soul. For instance, the emotion of sadness appears as an image of an older woman holding out a treasure chest which slowly opens. What is in the chest? Look inside. Why and how is it valuable to you? Next, ask the emotion what it desires to communicate to you at this time. Breathe deeply and record your impressions.

You will likely be surprised at the insights you glean from this exercise. Often, we must look beyond the surface of emotions to determine what lies beneath them. For instance, fear may hide under anger. Just as often, we may discover that our thoughts and beliefs need to be adjusted or released. In the case of persistent troubling thoughts, there are almost always underlying beliefs and thoughts that need to be examined, reworked, or released to move beyond them.

3. **Determine Patterns in Emotions:** On a sheet of paper or in your journal, write the troubling emotion as a heading. Then, close your eyes and recall the last time you felt the emotion. In a few words, write what was going on at this time. Were you interacting with anyone or alone? Did you see or hear something on TV or on the Internet that triggered the emotion? Did the pattern emerge at a particular event? Describe its intensity.

Once you recall this, allow your memory to drift to times *before* the most recent one when you felt the same emotion arise. Give details of the circumstances, events, and how you felt. When finished, compare the events when this same emotion manifested. What are the similarities? The differences? Is there a pattern that emerges? Accessing this helps you to make a game plan when you find yourself in similar situations that trigger the emotion. For example, if the emotion arises when you are in social situations, how can you best prepare for these? Create an action plan for each situation.

Experience the Bond of Love to Heal Grief

Losing a loved one is one of the most challenging events people face during life. The journey of grieving is as unique as the individual who undertakes it. There is no correct or incorrect way to grieve. Understanding that the soul and love are never destroyed by death provides assurance, comfort, and hope after loss.

This is the most beneficial aspect of mediumship, in my opinion. I have personally seen how the bond of love forever connects us with those who have returned home. I've also witnessed that those in spirit know about our thoughts and feelings because of this bond. They are not gone; they live on and are aware of our lives. The exercises in this section are designed to help you as you walk the pathway of grief.

1. **Dialogue with Your Loved One:** Find a photo of your loved one and place it in front of you. Go into a quiet place. Light a candle if you wish. Have paper and a pen beside you. As you gaze at the photo, imagine that you are having a conversation, as if this person is sitting across from you. What do you want to express? If there were words unexpressed during life, give voice to those now. Listen closely for intuitive impressions that come. (These may arise during the exercise or a short time later.)

   Now think about your relationship with your loved one. What were the positive aspects? What did you enjoy most? What lessons did your loved one bring to you? How was your life improved by their presence? Note: If there were painful or difficult aspects, you can explore these in the section for forgiveness below. When you feel complete, write your impressions to review later.

2. **Meditation to Meet with Your Loved One:** Go to a comfortable space, remove distractions, and close your eyes. After a few moments of focusing on your breath, imagine a white, shimmering column of light is directly in front of you. Within this light is safety, security, peace, and beauty. Feel it lifting you higher and higher. You touch down in a peaceful forest and find yourself standing on a pathway that leads deeper into the woods.

As you look into the distance, you see a white gazebo at the end of the pathway. This is a meeting place for you and your loved ones in spirit. Walk down the pathway and stand before the gazebo. You notice there are several comfortable seats inside; one is for you and the others for your loved ones.

Enter the gazebo and take a seat. Silently call your loved ones' names and invite them to join you now. In a few seconds, feel their presence embracing you, look into their eyes and express love. Feel that love being returned to you.

Now open your hands and heart to receive a gift from a loved one. This will come through an emotion, a symbol, an image, or a sensation in your body. It has meaning for your life right now.

Before departing, ask your loved ones to remain with you throughout the day. As you prepare to exit the gazebo, place the cherished gift to your heart. Return to the pathway and to the column of white light. Gently glide back to waking consciousness through the light. Breathe deeply and open your eyes.

3. **Ask for a Calling Card:** Many people have asked me how they can feel the presence of loved ones around them, *without a medium*. This exercise will help you connect with them and ask for a calling card — that is, a sensation, image, feeling, smell, or symbol which is the unique signature of your loved one. For instance, my mom in spirit has come to me by creating a tingling sensation on my right calf when I was meditating. When this initially happened, I sensed her presence with me. This is the only time when I receive this sensation and I know it is her personal signature when it occurs. If at first you don't receive the calling card, repeat the exercise several times.

Become comfortable and close your eyes. Focus on your breath and relax. Silently call upon your loved one(s) and ask them for a specific, unique sign that will alert you to their presence. Trust that they hear your request. Give thanks and return your attention to your breath before opening your eyes.

You can do this exercise as often as you desire until the calling card appears. Examples of calling cards are sensations in your body (such as the tingling mentioned above), smells associated with your loved ones (cologne, perfume, cigarette smoke, flowers, or a favorite food), an emotion suddenly washing over you, or an image or symbol. You may also receive calling cards through synchronistic occurrences, like the appearance of repeating numbers (such as 11:11), numbers associated with their birth or passing date, the repeated appearance of certain birds in your environment, their first name mentioned in conversation shortly after asking for a calling card, hearing your name being called upon going to sleep or waking, or electrical interruptions/disturbances in your home (lights flashing, TV going off and on, or "blank" phone calls with no one on the other end). Remember that your loved ones want to communicate with you as much as you do! When it comes to love, there is no separation between worlds.

Practices for Forgiveness

In previous writings, I've emphasized the significance of forgiveness as fundamental to the spiritual pathway. I've referred to it as the cornerstone of all healing.

To be clear, forgiveness, spiritually speaking, simply means a release of the past. People are often confused about what this indicates in the case of healing emotional wounds when they've been genuinely hurt by others. They mistakenly believe forgiveness indicates the hurt is condoned or accepted. This is *not* the true meaning of forgiveness. Rather, forgiveness means making a conscious choice to *release* the past wounds. By doing so, true emotional, mental, and spiritual liberation occur. The heaviness of the past disintegrates in the healing balm of forgiveness.

The only requirement to accomplish this is our conscious decision to do so. I once read that forgiveness is a selfish act because it is done for ourselves, not for those who have hurt us. I believe this to be true since we have no control over others. They may not be directly affected by our decision to forgive, but we assuredly are. We liberate ourselves from the burden of the past which frees us to be the best we can. The baggage is gone and we have peace within.

We've all experienced emotional hurt, rejection, disappointments, and unjust anger from others. The truth is that these projections can hurt us only if we allow them to. Often, when others lash out at us, they are experiencing their own frustrations, pain, and disappointments. In the moment, this is difficult for us to see and we may react in an equally hurtful manner. If we internalize the projections, they become lodged in our consciousness and cause damage to our sense of self-worth, our dignity, relationships, and our perceptions about the world.

A word needs to be said about self-forgiveness — one of the most significant actions we can take to improve our life. Through numerous sessions, I've connected with clients who regret not doing one thing or another in their relationships with deceased loved ones or in their own lives. At times, people carry these regrets for years without realizing how much these have corrupted or destroyed their inner peace. Stubbornly holding onto self-recriminations robs us of happiness and positive self-esteem; it separates us from the power of our own soul. Guilt, especially, distorts relationships with loved ones in spirit because it undermines the heart connection with them. We hold the faulty belief that we should have or could have done something differently, when this is not the case at all.

In numerous sessions I've done, souls have encouraged recipients of the readings to let go of self-blame and instead focus on the positive aspects of the relationship. Many times, guilt is born from our own misperceptions about others, the situation, or ourselves. For more information about the lingering effects of guilt after loss, see my book *Soul to Soul Connections: Comforting Messages from the Spirit World*.

If you are holding onto the past, make a decision to release it today. Place it in its proper perspective by concentrating on and being grateful for what you enjoy today, no matter how small. These exercises will help in that process.

1. **Gratitude as Forgiveness:** As in the earlier exercise on healing grief, place a photo of your loved one in front of you. Have paper and pen ready. Close your eyes and focus on your breath. Bring to mind what behaviors, actions, or words you have experienced pain, anger, or regret about in the relationship. These may have been initiated by your loved one in spirit or by you. Allow yourself to feel these and the accompanying emotions deeply. Do not push them away. After a few moments, open your eyes and write these on the paper.

   Next, refocus on your breath and close your eyes again. This time call forth as many positive aspects of the relationship as possible. If there are just a few, it's fine. Now reframe the emotional hurt as a conduit for your personal growth, instead of your pain. Feel it diminish in size through gratitude for that growth. Consider what you learned about yourself, in a positive manner, from the relationship. This may take a few moments or you may need to ponder this over time. Record these insights in your writing. If you do not yet feel ready to do this, come back to this exercise when you feel the time is right.

It's helpful to consider that we often give undue weight to the negative over the positive. When you pass into spirit, would you like to be remembered for your good or bad traits? Of course, you'd like people to recall the good about you. The same applies to loved ones who hurt you. Examine the entire relationship and determine three redeeming qualities of your loved one. It may take time for this shift in perspective to occur, yet it likely will.

2. **Exercise for Self-Forgiveness:** It's been stated many times that we are often our worst critics. In fact, we would likely not tolerate the criticism from others that we heap upon ourselves. The truth is, we all make mistakes, engage in less than admirable behavior and are far from perfect. If you recognize that you are engaging in this form of self-sabotage and unrealistic perfectionism, make the decision to change today.

Take a sheet of paper and draw a line down the middle. On one side, write a list of past hurts you routinely carry, that repeat in your mind or steal your inner peace. These may be regrets over something you said, did or those you *wish* you had said or done. In the case of guilt over something that occurred with a deceased loved one, write the incident in full, in all its detail.

On the other side of the paper, write as many positive, good qualities that you possess. Be gut-honest. It's often difficult for us to appreciate our favorable qualities when they are buried under guilt and self-loathing. List as many as you can during this exercise.

Now take a fair appraisal of both sides of your list. Chances are that the "good" list is much longer than the "bad" one. Often, we ignore these and instead give magnification to our perceived faults. Realize that each time we do this, we exalt these perceived weaknesses over the good attributes we possess.

Now that you can clearly see your positive character traits, embrace them. Each time self-recriminations arise, counter them by recalling several of the good. Practicing this will help you to recalibrate your self-image, raise your spiritual frequency, and release the past.

You Are Not Limited or Defined by Challenges

Within you lies everything you need to triumph over challenges because Spirit is within you. There is nothing else to obtain or know but the beauty, strength, and magnitude of your own soul. You are Spirit in a glorious form who has come to this physical plane to learn and grow.

This is the great adventure, the magical voyage, the joyride we all embark on. When difficulties inevitably occur, listen to, follow, and trust the wise whispers of your intuition — the higher guidance and wisdom of your soul and Spirit. And when the day arrives that you return home, you will see that through it all, you have been nourished and sustained by the great love of the Creator. This is the love you courageously came here to give and receive; it is the indestructible substance that is forever yours. It and service to others are all we take with us when leaving this earth.

Difficult times irrevocably transform us. They are the catalysts that invite us to explore the immortal terrain of our soul, peering deeply into every crevice, corner, top and bottom of our very being. No matter the nature of the difficulty, we will prevail by cradling ourselves in the soothing cocoon of Light within. The journey, the probing, and the scrutiny of ourselves grace life with meaning far beyond what we could imagine. We are never diminished, undermined, or defeated by distressing circumstances; we are strengthened by them. This is the richness of who we are. This is what we came here to do.

Perhaps this excerpt from one of my sessions sums it up best:

Miriam, a recent widow, asks, "I want to know exactly what took my husband Frank's life. He went to bed, and when I tried to wake him, he was gone. What could have happened to him? Why did this happen to me? I lie awake at night asking God to reveal this to me, but I don't get an answer. I'm angry and hurt. Why did he have to die? Can he tell you what happened?"

A clear impression forms in my mind. The simplicity of it stuns me.

"He says his death was like walking through a door, from one room to another. No more, no less. He floated above his body and his soul's exit was easy. He wants you to live your life knowing he is at peace and always with you."

I wait for Frank to elucidate his passing, but nothing comes about the nature of his death. I sense that this is not what matters now, at least from his soul's perspective. But he leaves a powerful final message with his widow before the communication ends:

"He says to read the words in the embroidered plaque that hangs on the wall of your kitchen."

I have no idea what this means, but I trust that Miriam does.

"Oh, heavens!" Miriam exclaims through tears. "A year ago, he bought me a plaque with the words, 'Joy be with you as you stay; Peace be with you on your way.'"

Throughout your soul's captivating adventure, may you find joy and may you be at peace ... now and always.

End Notes

Chapter 1

1. Mcleod, Saul, PhD. "What Is Cognitive Dissonance Theory?" simplepsychology.org/cognitive-dissonance.html, 2023, citing Festinger, Leon, *A Theory of Cognitive Dissonance*. Stanford, California: Stanford University Press (Anniversary edition), 1957.
2. Ware, Bronnie. *The Top Five Regrets of the Dying: A Life Transformed by the Dearly Departing*. Carlsbad, California: Hay House, 2019.

Chapter 3

1. KFF. "Latest Federal Data Show That Young People Are More Likely Than Older Adults to Be Experiencing Symptoms of Anxiety or Depression." (March 20, 2023). San Francisco, California: kff.org.
2. Emoto, Masaru. *The Hidden Messages in Water*. New York, New York: Atria Books (Illustrated edition), 2005.

Chapter 4

1. Hayes, Patricia. *Extension of Life: Arthur Ford Speaks*. Georgia: Dimensional Brotherhood Publishing House, 1986.

Chapter 5

1. St. John of the Cross (Juan de Yepes y Álvarez), translation by David Lewis. *The Dark Night of the Soul*. Poetryfoundation. org, 2023.
2. Anonymous. *The Big Book of Alcoholics Anonymous*, 4th edition. New York, New York: Alcoholics Anonymous World Services, Inc., 2002.

Chapter 6

1. Plato. *Republic*. A Socratic dialogue written circa 375 BC.

Recommended Books

Arroyo, Stephen. *Astrology, Karma & Transformation: The Inner Dimensions of the Birth Chart*. Sebastopol, California: CRCS Publications, 2013.

Arroyo, Stephen. *Chart Interpretation Handbook: Guidelines for Understanding the Essentials of the Birth Chart*. California: CRCS Publications, 2004.

Bear Heart and Larkin, Molly. *The Wind Is My Mother: The Life and Teachings of a Native American Shaman*. New York: Berkley Books, 1998.

Green, Jeffrey Wolf and Green, Deva (ed.). *Evolutionary Astrology*. Independently published, 2019.

Green, Jeffrey Wolf. *Pluto: The Evolutionary Journey of the Soul, Volume 1*. Swanage, England: The Wessex Astrologer, 2011.

Teal, Celeste. *Lunar Nodes: Discover Your Soul's Karmic Mission*. Woodbury, Minnesota: Llewellyn Publications, 2008.

Tolle, Eckhart. *A New Earth: Awakening to Your Life's Purpose*. New York, New York: Penguin Life, 2005.

Vega, Phyllis and Macgregor, Trish. *Power Tarot: More Than 100 Spreads That Give Specific Answers to Your Most Important Questions*. New York, New York: Atria Books, 1998.

Williams, Mark and Penman, Danny. *Mindfulness: An Eight-Week Plan for Finding Peace in a Frantic World*. Emmaus, Pennsylvania: Rodale Books, Reprint edition, 2012.

Also by carole j. obley

Embracing the Ties That Bind: Connecting with Spirit
(ISBN: 1-4010-8971-2)
*I'm Still with You: True Stories of Healing Grief Through Spirit
Communication*
(ISBN: 978-1-84694-107-8)
*Soul to Soul Connections: Comforting Messages from the Spirit
World*
(ISBN: 978-1-84694-967-8)
*Wisdom From the Spirit World: Life Teachings on Love, Forgiveness,
Purpose and Finding Peace*
(ISBN: 978-1-78904-302-0)

About the Author

Acclaimed spiritual medium and popular author carole j. obley has been the bridge between heaven and earth in more than 14,000 group and individual readings. Names, descriptions of loved ones' personalities, and uncanny, validating details — as well as grief support and teachings about the afterlife — are typically delivered in her sessions.

An advanced intuitive, Carole also regularly delivers specific, practical guidance in readings about a wide variety of life issues, including relationships, business, and spirituality. She is recognized by clients for bringing compassion and integrity to mediumship via her sincere intent to be of service to others.

Carole is a regular guest on George Noory's *Coast to Coast* radio show, as well as numerous other media, where she offers interviews and live on-air readings. In addition to maintaining a private practice in mediumship nationally, she presents seminars and workshops in person and through online teachings. Carole has taught many workshops at Lilydale, NY, the largest US center for Spiritualism. Her previous four books have been well received by a reading audience worldwide.

She may be contacted through her website: Soulvisions.net.

6TH
BOOKS

ALL THINGS PARANORMAL

Investigations, explanations and deliberations on the
paranormal, supernatural, explainable or unexplainable.
6th Books seeks to give answers while nourishing the soul:
whether making use of the scientific model or anecdotal and
fun, but always beautifully written.
Titles cover everything within parapsychology: how to,
lifestyles, alternative medicine, beliefs, myths and theories.
If you have enjoyed this book, why not tell other readers by
posting a review on your preferred book site?

Spirit Release
Sue Allen
A guide to psychic attack, curses, witchcraft, spirit attachment,
possession, soul retrieval, haunting, deliverance, exorcism and
more, as taught at the College of Psychic Studies.
Paperback: 978-1-84694-033-0 ebook: 978-1-84694-651-6

Advanced Psychic Development
Becky Walsh
Learn how to practise as a professional, contemporary
spiritual medium.
Paperback: 978-1-84694-062-0 ebook: 978-1-78099-941-8

Where After
Mariel Forde Clarke
A journey that will compel readers to view life after
death in a completely different way.
Paperback: 978-1-78904-617-5 ebook: 978-1-78904-618-2

Poltergeist! A New Investigation into Destructive Haunting
John Fraser
Is the Poltergeist "syndrome" the only type of paranormal
phenomena that can really be proven?
Paperback: 978-1-78904-397-6 ebook: 978-1-78904-398-3

A Little Bigfoot: On the Hunt in Sumatra
Pat Spain
Pat Spain lost a layer of skin, pulled leeches off his nether regions, and was violated by an Orangutan for this book.
Paperback: 978-1-78904-605-2 ebook: 978-1-78904-606-9

Astral Projection Made Easy
and overcoming the fear of death
Stephanie June Sorrell
From the popular Made Easy series, *Astral Projection Made Easy* helps to eliminate the fear of death through discussion of life beyond the physical body.
Paperback: 978-1-84694-611-0 ebook: 978-1-78099-225-9

Haunted: Horror of Haverfordwest
G.L. Davies
Blissful beginnings for a young couple turn into a nightmare after purchasing their dream home in Wales in 1989.
Paperback: 978-1-78535-843-2 ebook: 978-1-78535-844-9

Readers of ebooks can buy or view any of these bestsellers by clicking on the live link in the title. Most titles are published in paperback and as an ebook. Paperbacks are available in traditional bookshops. Both print and ebook formats are available online.

Find more titles and sign up to our readers' newsletter at
www.6th-books.com

Join the 6th books Facebook group at
6th Books The world of the Paranormal